A
CHARGE
TO
KEEP

A
CHARGE
TO
KEEP

The Life of Earl Gladstone Hunt, Jr.

JAMES C. LOGAN

ABINGDON PRESS
Nashville

A CHARGE TO KEEP
The Life of Earl Gladstone Hunt, Jr.

Copyright © 2000 by Abingdon Press

This book is printed on recycled, acid-free, elemental-chlorine–free paper.

Library of Congress Cataloging in Publication Data

Logan, James C.
    A charge to keep : the life of Earl Gladstone Hunt, Jr. / James C. Logan.
      p. cm.
    Includes bibliographical references and index,
    ISBN 0-687-03397-7 (alk. paper)
    1. Hunt, Earl G. 2. United Methodist Church (U.S.)—Bishops—Biography. I. Title.

BX8495.H827 L64 2000
287'.6'092—dc21
[B]   99-086403

00 01 02 03 04 05 06 07 08 09—10 9 8 7 6 5 4 3 2 1

MANUFACTURED IN THE UNITED STATES OF AMERICA

To Those

Congregations and Pastors

of

Four Annual Conferences

Western North Carolina

Memphis

Tennessee

Florida

Who Shared with Their Bishop in a Mutual Ministry

of

Witness to Jesus Christ

Acknowledgments

*T*he telling of the story of Earl Gladstone Hunt Jr. has been truly a collaborative effort. Without the generous assistance of many persons—former parishioners, colleague pastors and bishops, administrators and faculty of Emory and Henry College, and a host of Earl Hunt's friends—this volume would not have been possible. To those who gave of their time and opened the storehouse of memories, I am indebted. I hope that they find not only their words but themselves faithfully presented in these pages.

To the Foundation for Evangelism goes special recognition for commissioning this project. John Marshall, former chairperson of the board, and Roy Warren, current chairperson, have been patient when progress was slow and have been encouraging when spirits needed lifting. Bishop Ernest Fitzgerald, president of the foundation, and Paul Ervin, executive vice president, have in good faith and good humor prodded me on. The United Methodist Church is especially gifted with the foundation. It does so much in the interest of evangelism in the church, particularly in the United Methodist theological schools. To cite only one example, the financial support that the foundation expends annually to underwrite the E. Stanley Jones professorships of evangelism in the United Methodist theological schools in this country and in Germany and Zimbabwe is staggering. The scope of the work that the foundation does with its various projects could never be replicated by boards and commissions of the church. The foundation does a supplementary work lying beyond the bounds of the mandated responsibilities of the General Board of Discipleship, and without this expanded ministry the church would be significantly impoverished. The foundation's action in honoring Bishop Hunt as he retired from the presidency of the foundation is indicative of the deep appreciation for a retired bishop who refused to retire and subsequently gave the foundation seven of its finest years.

To two persons I must give singular recognition. Robert F. Lundy, who was elected to the episcopacy in Malaysia in 1964 (the same year Hunt was elected) and Hunt's longtime friend, did much of the initial research in interviews. Lundy and Hunt are native Holstonians and were classmates at Candler School of Theology. "Wiz," Bob's wife, rendered invaluable service at the computer. Bob and "Wiz" will find their footprints across these pages time and time again. Without their efforts this project would not have been possible.

Daniel G. Leidig, former dean of Emory and Henry College, has written the poetic interpretation of Hunt as preacher that prefaces the chapter on preaching. Dan gave me a long afternoon of his time to deepen my understanding of Hunt's academic administration at Emory and Henry College, and he subsequently supplied me with documentary resources.

On my home front of Wesley Theological Seminary, I appreciate beyond words the careful readings and wise comments of Douglass Lewis, president, and David McAllister-Wilson, executive vice president. They have been my "fog index," prompting me to lighten an acquired Germanic density of expression. Suzanne Gibson Vance has been my diligent guide to the intricacies of computer technology of which I am a mere novice.

Of all persons, I owe special gratitude to Mary Ann and Earl

Hunt. They have given me all the assistance for which I asked and with amazing grace tolerated my intrusions into their home and time. Beyond the writing of this volume, they have been special friends since 1963.

To the many people, a list far too long to include, with whom I have had conversations in person, by mail, and by telephone, I acknowledge my indebtedness. Their memories, anecdotes, and comments appear frequently without attribution but not without my deep appreciation.

The "biographic moment" occurs when various kinds of stories and narratives converge in a single life story. I am grateful for the many storytellers, named and unnamed, who have contributed to this story.

Contents

Foreword *13*

Preface *17*

Chapter One Beginnings *21*

Chapter Two Pastor *41*

Chapter Three College President *50*

Chapter Four Episcopacy *68*

Chapter Five Bridge Builder *113*

Chapter Six Preacher *141*

Chapter Seven Evangelist *164*

Chapter Eight Educator *188*

Chapter Nine Believer *207*

Epilogue *224*

Notes *231*

Index *241*

Foreword

$\mathcal{I}$n his life and work, Earl Gladstone Hunt Jr. embodies all that is best in Christian ministry. As a student in the East Tennessee State University and Candler School of Theology at Emory University, he gave evidence of the brilliant mind that epitomized his entire career. As a pastor, he brought to the pulpit a splendid combination of sound theology, biblical insight, and oratorical skills that early marked him for distinction. His years as president of Emory and Henry College revealed his lifelong passion for the combination of the Wesleyan model, "knowledge and vital piety." As a youthful bishop in the church, he used his ability in administration and preaching to stimulate annual conferences to new visions and accomplishments. As a more mature episcopal leader, he gave evidence of church statesmanship that caught the attention of worldwide Methodism.

Earl Hunt's ministry has made a difference! He moved conferences to bold ventures, such as appointing the first African American minister to the district superintendency in the Southeastern Jurisdiction. He led in evangelistic endeavors and in strengthening the role of church-related higher education. His innovating role set the pace for the more efficient work of a bishop by being the first in the Southeastern Jurisdiction to create the office of Administrative Assistant to the Bishop, and Lay Advisory Council for the Bishop. His indefatigable labors in being present with pastors, their families, and local churches enabled him to strengthen the appointive process and to lead in the solution in points of conflict between lay and clergy.

Earl Hunt's long and effective leadership brought him in the closing years of his episcopacy to the presidency of the Council of Bishops of The United Methodist Church, which position he held with dignity and strength.

In all of his crowded days as a bishop, he still found time to continue to read and write. His book *A Bishop Speaks His Mind,* although seen by some as controversial at points, captured the attention of the church and was a source of inspiration and hope to many of Methodism's world-embracing constituency.

In his years of retirement, Earl Hunt has vividly highlighted his major concern—"the winning of disciples to our Lord Jesus Christ." In his presidency of the Foundation for Evangelism, he has brought new emphasis and programmatic support for the renewal of our major mission of bringing hope and healing to a lost world in the name of our Lord and Savior, Jesus Christ.

It is fitting that Dr. James C. Logan, a longtime associate of Bishop Hunt, should give us interesting and personal insights into a life and ministry that have made a significant difference in our Methodism and in Christendom.

Edward L. Tullis
Retired Bishop of
The United Methodist Church

A
CHARGE
TO
KEEP

Preface

❦

To be human is to tell stories. Humankind not only thrives on but literally lives by telling stories. Biography is a special kind of story, a richly textured blend of varied kinds of story. Within the complexity of the variety of stories is found the family story. The family narrative is basic in supplying initial chronology, and as in the story of Earl G. Hunt Jr., the family story is laden with the basic values that characterize his entire life. Yet the family story is lived within a cultural story, the larger environmental story that provides the historical and cultural placement of the family story. In the case of Earl Hunt, the ecclesial or church's story must be given particular attention. Here the biblical and Wesleyan evangelical traditions play formative roles. And other stories—educational, institutional, collegial— must be told to render a full biographical story.

In this particular instance, the biographical story of Earl G. Hunt Jr. would be impossible to narrate without the pervasive faith story or Christian story. Composed of the scriptural story, the church's story of tradition, and the life stories of individual Christians, the faith story knits together and holds all the little stories in the life narrative of Earl Hunt. The faith story is the big story (what literary commentators call the metastory) that supplies the consuming motive and the integrative cohesion of the rich personal story. In other words, the faith story brings all the other stories into one single, focused story.

Many forces in a so-called postmodern world tempt us to distrust the telling of stories, especially the metastory of faith. My hope is that the telling of Bishop Hunt's story will be a reminder to us that storytelling is essential to human life. We live in stories, and Christian faith is nurtured and sustained when we see in human flesh and blood a life lived within the Christian story. Perhaps in the telling of his story we may capture something of the evangelical zeal that animates his story. Whether in proclamation, evangelism, or administration his passion was always to tell "the Story."

> I love to tell the story of unseen things above
>   of Jesus and his glory, of Jesus and his love.
> I love to tell the story, because I know 'tis true;
>   it satisfies my longings as nothing else can do.

> I love to tell the story, 'twill be my theme in glory,
>   to tell the old, old story of Jesus and his love.[1]

I first met Earl Hunt on a misty spring morning in 1963 at the Tri-Cities Airport in East Tennessee. Hunt had called me from Massachusetts to interview for a teaching position at Emory and Henry College. I had recently returned from doctoral studies in Switzerland, and it had been necessary for me to have major surgery. My doctor permitted me to make the trip on the condition that I promise not to lift as much as a briefcase. I can still see this distinguished gentleman working his way through the airport parking lot carrying a briefcase in one hand and a suitcase in the other.

In June of 1964 I assumed the pastorate of the Emory Methodist Church, the college-community church, while continuing to teach in the college. My appointment to the pastorate of the church technically made me Hunt's pastor when he was elected to the episcopacy! Since those days he and I have crossed paths in various arenas of the church's life.

When the Foundation for Evangelism asked me to write this biography, I accepted with considerable ambivalence. Hunt is one of the figures in the church whom I have held in highest regard for thirty-five years. Of course, I wanted to join the foundation in its recognition of Bishop Hunt. On the other hand, my academic training has been that of a systematic theologian, not a historian. To think that I could write a biography was and still is an audacious assumption.

Across thirty-three years of teaching in a United Methodist theological seminary I have become increasingly convinced of and convicted by Methodism's peculiar ecclesiology. Wesleyans were a mission movement long before they became a church. And when they took action to become a church, first in 1784, they did so for missional reasons. Rather than deriving mission from church, Wesleyans derived church from mission. Mission is, therefore, for Methodists the one indispensable mark of the church. Forsake mission and we forsake the rationale for our existence as a church. Mission has varied forms. Evangelism, social reform, and the global growth of the church are but three dimensions of mission. David Bosch's analogy that evangelism is to mission what the heart is to the human body is a fitting one.[2] Few people in the contemporary United Methodist Church have expressed and embodied Bosch's analogy more than Earl Hunt.

As I read the books, letters, and papers of Bishop Hunt, I have been impressed, as will be plainly evident to the reader of this volume, with Hunt's character as it was shaped by the particular evangelical culture in which he was reared. Southern Methodist evangelicalism is a distinctive hue within the larger mosaic of

Protestant evangelicalism. It is a conjunctive tradition nurtured with personal piety, communal faith, and a passion that the grace of Jesus Christ be shared with all people. It is a tradition that abhors the antithesis of irreconcilable opposites and will not rest at ease with a compromise for a synthesis that sacrifices the truth of both thesis and antithesis. Mind and heart, personal and social, faith and action are held in creative tension. This, the tradition claimed, was possible because the grace of the Lord Jesus Christ is the only power capable of embracing the diversity of the human race and unifying the race into a reconciled Body of Christ.

My thesis is not that Hunt was deterministically shaped by the forces of his cultural and ecclesial environment. He freely accepted his tradition without idolizing it and attempted to employ his tradition in bridging the chasms of the modern church. In tracing Hunt's roots, I have discovered something of my own. My family history is situated in the same valley as his, though on the Virginia side of the state line. This venture has been, to use Donald Dayton's words, no less than a "discovering of an evangelical heritage."[3]

Hunt's personal faith, which he proclaimed publicly with considerable rhetorical skill, was an Incarnation-anchored, Cross-centered, resurrection faith. The closing words of one of his writings offer an appropriate introduction to his life and ministry: "So it is that, for the Christian, the gloom and despair of life's burdens and issues are suddenly shattered by the crashing chords of resurrection truth and promise. . . . My confidence, and I hope yours as well, is in the resurrection faith, to which I witness gratefully and gladly before the world."[4]

Chapter One

Beginnings

The one hundred forty-sixth session of the Florida
Annual Conference was fast approaching adjournment.
On this warm May 1988 afternoon Bishop Earl G. Hunt Jr.
was presiding over the final annual conference session of his
twenty-four-year tenure as a bishop of The United Methodist
Church. Earlier in the week he had addressed the conference
with a forward-looking state-of-the-church address entitled
"When All Things Become New." In July at the jurisdictional
conference a new bishop would be assigned to the Florida Area,
and Bishop Hunt would retire from the effective episcopacy.

Few bishops are elected at the young age of forty-five, and
few experience a tenure of twenty-four years. Even fewer bishops serve through periods of such momentous change. Bishop
William Grove has commented:

> His service in the office has spanned one of the most turbulent
> and dramatic periods in our nation's history: the period in which
> we have struggled for the soul of the nation and the civil rights
> movement, the war in Vietnam, the so-called sexual revolution,
> and the increasing secularization of our society. During this peri-
> od The United Methodist Church, the most "national" of our
> churches, has witnessed valiantly, even heroically, to the relevance
> of the gospel to these social challenges. But during this same peri-
> od the church has decreased in membership and today experi-
> ences the pain of conflicting opinions and confused identity.[1]

The Hunt family's roots are embedded in upper East Tennessee and western North Carolina. The South Holston River courses its way from southwestern Virginia into eastern Tennessee with the haze-covered Smokies to the east and the rolling Tennessee hills to the west. Settlers of staunch Scotch-Irish descent streamed into this territory in the last quarter of the eighteenth century. This was the wilderness with the population centered in the area today known as the Tri-Cities (Bristol, Kingsport, and Johnson City).

Francis Asbury had become aware of the Holston Valley through Methodist settlers like Edward Cox, whose house stands today as a reminder in Bluff City, Tennessee. As early as 1783 Asbury had appointed Jeremiah Lambert to establish a circuit. Bishop Asbury himself conducted a conference of the western preachers at Keywood, near Saltville, Virginia, in 1788. When young William McKendree arrived in 1800 to take up the task of presiding elder, Methodism was advancing numerically and institutionally primarily through the means of camp meeting evangelism.

The Hunts did not "come by" their Methodism accidentally. Their geographical location had been prime Methodist territory for generations. In fact, Earl Hunt's father was born in Sulphur Springs, Tennessee, a site of one of the early annual camp meetings, and the future bishop as a youth attended many preaching services at the old Sulphur Springs Camp Meeting.

Earl Gladstone Hunt Jr. was born on September 14, 1918, in Johnson City, Tennessee, just weeks before the Armistice ending World War I was signed. His father, Earl Hunt Sr., from the tiny town of Sulphur Springs, had received only eight years of formal education. In his adult years the elder Hunt worked as a drummer or traveling salesman for the Summers Hardware and Supply Company in Johnson City. His sales circuit took him from East Tennessee into western North Carolina. His son, Earl

Jr., remembers with affection his father as "unostentatious about his religion, but he went to church regularly and supported the church as generously as his limited income allowed."[2] During the depression, he lost all his meager savings but refused to take bankruptcy and paid off every penny of his indebtedness before suffering a heart attack.

When Earl Jr. became the bishop of the Charlotte Area in 1964, many people in that region had known his father well and had held him in high regard. The bishop tells of speaking at a large Marion District rally held in the Bakersville, North Carolina, high school auditorium in 1965. Dr. A. Glenn Lackey was the host district superintendent. At the close of the service there were six stalwart overall-clad mountain men waiting to speak to their bishop. Their spokesman said: "So, you're Earl's boy, are you? Son, we loved your daddy, and we don't love easy."

While escorting the bishop to his motel that evening, Dr. Lackey made a sage comment: "Bishop, it's fortunate that your daddy was a good man; if he hadn't been, you'd be ruined in the Western North Carolina Conference!"[3]

Young Hunt's mother hailed from Asheville, North Carolina; she was the daughter of a pharmacist who died in the influenza epidemic of 1888. Following her father's death, Tommie Mae DeVault was taken by her widowed mother to live near relatives in Jonesborough, Tennessee. In Jonesborough, now a young woman, Tommie Mae met Earl G. Hunt, and they were married on October 12, 1912. Tommie Mae had completed her high school education in Jonesborough, and throughout her married life she maintained and supervised a scrupulously polished home for her husband and son. She became a lover of learning and culture and passed the passion to her son.

During the depression of 1929, she raised flowers, and it was her son's responsibility to assist with the grocery bill by selling

the flowers in the community. The Hunts managed to make ends meet and somehow found fifty cents a week for their young son's allowance. His mother's love for learning no doubt was the influence that led him to spend his allowance on books, though an incongruous mixture was his selection, consisting of Tom Swift, Charles Dickens, the Rover Boys, and Mark Twain.

His devoted parents and the affections of an extended family nurtured young Earl. Uncle Homer and Aunt Ann lived in the old family home place at Sulphur Springs along with Aunt Nell, and their home was a hospitable retreat. Uncle Bill and Aunt Clara lived in Johnson City. Uncle Bruce, a public educator for forty years in South Carolina's Low Country, stimulated his nephew's vision for a sound education. Grandfather Hunt, like most of the Hunt family, was an ardent Methodist. He never missed the sessions of the annual conference of the Methodist Episcopal Church. Grandson Earl often accompanied his grandfather to conference, and the elder Hunt would never have considered leaving the final session of conference without conversing with "his bishop."

Unquestionably, the intertwining mix of family and church, home and religion, provided the major life-shaping and character-forming environment of the younger Hunt as he grew and matured. The Tennessee Valley, like much of the Southland, abounded in Christian piety generally known as evangelical Protestantism. For generations the Hunts had lived in and were nourished by the evangelical faith as proclaimed, taught, and lived by their church, which was the Methodist Episcopal Church (commonly referred to as "the northern church").

Southern evangelicalism is a variegated religious phenomenon and does not lend itself to facile definition. Southern Presbyterians, with their high consciousness of Calvinist doctrine, tend toward a more cognitive faith, seeing the essence of

Christianity as the preaching and practice of divinely revealed biblical truth. The radical expression of this is fundamentalism. Southern Baptists, on the other hand, move more in the direction of an experiential, conversionist approach to faith, emphasizing personal conversion and "born again" religion. Brothers and sisters in the Methodist connection demonstrate a pietism of "heart religion," stressing a devotional religion focused on and living by the Lord's intimate and constant presence. Obviously, such descriptions are generalizations, and there is considerable crossover. Nevertheless the Methodism that nurtured Hunt was distinctive in its emphasis on a constant "walking with the Lord" and living out the "walk" in loving service to the neighbor.[4]

The Methodists were identified not so much by content of doctrine as by warmness of heart. For Methodists, as for Baptists, conversion religion was important and was punctuated with the annual camp meeting or local church revival. But for Methodists, conversion was always accompanied by the call to the day-to-day walk with the Lord. Throughout the year, the major energy of the church focused on undergirding the ongoing life of personal religion. Methodists could absorb a variety of doctrinal nuances from one pastorate to another as long as the ethos of heart religion was sustained. They were ecumenically open and enthusiastically cooperative with other denominations whose love of the Lord Jesus was the same as theirs. Such was the evangelical context into which Hunt was born and which nourished his young faith.

This is vividly illustrated by the two pastors who influenced him most in his childhood and youth. Hunt was baptized as an infant and after confirmation was received into membership in the First Methodist Episcopal Church of Johnson City. Dr. Joseph Warren Broyles came to the pastorate of First Church with impeccable scholarly credentials and a social passion for those struggling in the poverty occasioned by the Great Depression. Broyles had been a Rhodes Scholar at Oxford and had earned a Ph.D. under the Methodist theologian Edwin Lewis at Drew University. Theologically, he embraced a position that could be called "evangelical liberalism." In later years Hunt recounted the infectious charm and incisive intellect of Broyles, but what was more important, "his eager commitment to God suffused my youthful soul with a desire to turn the world upside down for Jesus Christ."[5] Broyles was later to become a professor at the Methodist Hamline University in Minneapolis and then president of West Virginia Wesleyan College.

Broyles's social passion inspired the youth of First Church to volunteer to work in a depressed area of the town known as Keystone Community. This youth ministry was called the Junior Mission. Through First Church the depression victims of the community were assisted in securing employment, and in particular, the youth endeavored to meet the needs of the children and youth. Hunt describes his early experiences in this social ministry:

> The church plant had a splendid gymnasium and to it the children of the factory community were brought after school twice a week for a vigorous athletic program, dramatically overdue shower baths, a brief Bible class, visits to a circulating library, a medical clinic and a soup kitchen. Regular pastoral visits into the homes from which the children came were instituted, and cottage prayer meetings complete with a Peter Bilhorn folding pump organ were begun. Food, fuel, clothing and medicine were distributed; and a highly effective employment bureau was founded. Church officials undertook conversations with factory and mill owners and city government officials, looking toward the facing of basic problems. Transportation to and from Sunday

services was provided, and a carefully groomed, somewhat self-centered middle-class Methodist church suddenly found in its midst a shabbily clothed, not always freshly washed, contingent of men and women and children who had only pennies for the offering plates but who could sing the old songs with more gusto than the congregational natives![6]

This experience fostered in him an early interest in the sociology of poverty and the economic mandates of the Christian gospel, concerns that he would not forget in later ministry.

During his college years at East Tennessee State College (later University), Hunt was impressed with another pastor of a quite different theological persuasion. Dr. Marshall L. Gamble, a graduate of Asbury Theological Seminary and recipient of an honorary degree from the same institution, was appointed to First Church. Dr. Gamble was shaped and formed by the holiness tradition that originated with the holiness revivals beginning in the 1830s in American Methodism. Theirs was the self-conscious attempt to recover the Wesleyan doctrine of entire sanctification or perfection (called by holiness people "the second blessing"), the loss of which they perceived to be the root cause of the church's diminishing evangelical zeal. The emphasis on the second blessing entailed both theologically and experientially two decisive or crisis experiences in the life of the Christian—conversion (justification) and the second blessing (entire sanctification or perfection). In comparison with Broyles, Gamble was a theological conservative with strong emphases on personal evangelism. In his senior year at East Tennessee State, Hunt was invited by Dr. Gamble to be the assistant to the pastor. Beginning to be shaped in the young man's mind and spirit was the fusion of evangelistic zeal and social conscience that would mark his future ministry.

Another person of influence, a laywoman, left her stamp on Hunt's youthful years. Mrs. Emily Miller Barlow, widow of a prominent attorney and daughter of a local physician, for four decades conducted Bible studies for the religious community of Johnson City. Mrs. Barlow was unquestionably of fundamentalist theological persuasion, staunchly teaching from the premise of biblical inerrancy. She combined her teaching abilities with a warm and winsome personal faith. In his contacts with her the youthful Hunt was impressed with the conviction that the primacy of Scripture was the basis for the Christian life. Although in later years he would be introduced to the methods of historical criticism in the interpretation of Scripture and he did not embrace the first tenet of fundamentalism, he retained the strong conviction of the centrality of Scripture for Christian faith and practice.

During the Johnson City years, Andy Bolinger entered the life of the young Hunt. Andy was a recovering alcoholic doomed to an early death because of the physical ravages of his dissipation. Through the ministry of First Church, Andy found Christ and became the probation officer for the local juvenile court. Andy was at the very center of First Church's mission to the poor of Johnson City. In the Junior Mission Hunt and Bolinger bonded and became close friends. "I can still recall," remembers Hunt, "the exhilarating contagion of Andy's laughter and a certain strange and wonderful light in Andy's eyes, which I have never seen anywhere else on earth."

On a cold, wet autumn afternoon Andy took fifty underprivileged children to the Ringling Brothers and Barnum and Bailey Circus. The exposure to the elements of weather brought an onslaught of pneumonia from which Andy, in his already weakened condition, would not recover. Still vivid in the memory of Hunt is the scene of the thronged sanctuary of First Church the afternoon of his memorial service. In the overflow crowd were to be seen a former governor of the state, the mayor of the city, and judges of local and district courts, intermingled with the boys and girls and their parents from the poverty-stricken area where Andy had struggled to bring a ray of light. The funeral procession on the way to Happy Valley Cemetery was more than three miles long! Two factors in this scene made indelible impressions on Hunt. First, he could not forget the tear-stained faces of the children of poverty. And, second, he could never erase the memory of Andy, who managed to gather the tattered fragments of his life into a ministry in which he literally lived and died for the children of poverty.[7]

Another strong influence, an ecumenical experience, came into play in these youthful years. A Johnson City Youth Council composed of young people from twenty-nine different churches ranging from the Protestant Episcopal Church to the Salvation Army gathered for a series of student-sponsored prayer meetings. Soon the prayer meetings expanded into a citywide program of youth rallies held each month during the academic year, featuring well-known Christian leaders of the period. Hunt was one of three young people founding the Youth Council. The young people were guided and advised by clergy of the city. Without ever paying an honorarium these young people brought to the city such prominent figures as Robert E. Speer, Peter Marshall, M. E. Dodd, Harold Paul Sloan, Dr. Howard Atwood Kelly, Dr. James Park McCallie, Bishop Edwin Holt Hughes, and Dr. E. Schuyler English. The rallies attracted thousands, young and old, and became a major event in the city's public life. From the ranks of the Youth Council more than thirty young people went into full-time Christian service around the world. The rallies were precursors of what would become in midcentury the annual Tri-Cities Preaching Mission, an ecumenical endeavor drawing leading preachers from across the country to Johnson City, Kingsport, and Bristol for a week of intensive ecumenical preaching events.

Among the guest speakers who came to the Youth Council's monthly rallies was the popular novelist Grace Livingston Hill. The power of her message and personality profoundly affected the young Hunt during a very impressionable time in his life. The two, a novelist and a preacher, were to remain friends through future years. Years after the Johnson City Youth Rally, Grace Livingston Hill called Hunt to inform him that she was sending him a copy of her new novel, *The Seventh Hour,* and then laughed as she informed him that she had used his name for the name of the villain in the plot![8]

In addition to these influences another development was occurring that in many ways would have an even weightier impact upon his life. Beginning in the fifth grade in elementary school and through succeeding years until college graduation, Earl had known Mary Ann Kyker. Childhood friendship blossomed into courtship and eventually into marriage. Mary Ann was one of five children, three girls and two boys, of Dr. and Mrs. Charles Hartsell Kyker. Mary Ann's father was a physician, and her mother was a registered nurse. Johnson City folk relate a familiar sight when after school hours Earl would carry Mary Ann's books for her and would engage in conversation with her by walking ahead, turning to face her as he walked.[9]

When Mary Ann was only thirteen years old, her mother died. Then at the age of twenty-two, she experienced the death of her father. The death of her mother left five siblings in the Kyker household. During her teens Mary Ann shouldered major family responsibilities while achieving academic merit in her schoolwork. She continued her studies beyond high school, graduating from East Tennessee State with a major in elementary education. She even managed to carve out time for participation in dramatic activities, which became a lifelong interest. Family responsibilities, academic studies, and avocational interests did not preclude the continuing and growing attraction of Earl and Mary Ann for each other.

On the afternoon of June 15, 1943, First Church was the scene of a wedding. Mary Ann Kyker and Earl G. Hunt Jr. were joined in holy matrimony. First Church was the faith-home of both the Kyker and the Hunt families. Like Earl, Mary Ann had grown up through Sunday school, confirmation, and Epworth League in the same church. In her youth Mary Ann had experienced a deeply meaningful experience of grace in the First Church of the United Brethren in Johnson City where the Reverend G. G. Richardson was pastor. In those days in local communities Methodists and United Brethren commonly enjoyed close relationships. Methodists and United Brethren could worship and serve together without any sense of spiritual discontinuity or denominational competition. That was a harbinger of days to come when in 1968 Earl would find himself a bishop of a newly united church of Methodists and Evangelical United Brethren. Mary Ann simply integrated her spiritual experience into her ongoing faith pilgrimage in First Methodist Church. She was gifted with exciting exuberance for life, undergirded by a long-nurtured, deep Christian piety. Mary Ann was not one to indulge in piosity and ostentation; the roots of her piety had nevertheless grown from the same soil of Methodist heart religion as had Earl's. She became his constant companion in the pastoral ministry. Their marriage began a new chapter extending over more than fifty years of a shared ministry. In 1980 Hunt dedicated his second full-length book to his wife and companion in ministry with these words of affection:

To Mary Ann
whose love, faith, and life
have lightened my load
and
brightened my way.[10]

Mary Ann and Earl moved to Atlanta, where Earl had already completed two years of his theological education at Candler School of Theology. The newlyweds settled into an apartment above the garage of the home of Bishop and Mrs. Arthur J. Moore. While Earl studied theology, Mary Ann taught in the elementary school system of Decatur.

Mary Ann accompanied her new husband to his student pastorate in the Buckhead community in Atlanta where, when schedules permitted, she quietly ministered alongside him, bringing the presence of her distinctive personality. Years later, as a bishop, Hunt recalled one such occasion when Mary Ann went with him in the middle of the night to the home of an elderly member of the little church he was serving. The person was dying. It was at the height of winter and a fierce blizzard was in process, so the drive in the ramshackle old car took more than an hour and a half. When at last the couple stood in the door of the parishioner's room, he looked up at them and said in feeble tones, "You cared enough to come!" After Earl had completed his work at the seminary and the Hunts had moved back to Holston, Mary Ann continued the same supportive ministry.

When Hunt became president of Emory and Henry College, Mary Ann developed a new dimension of her ministry. She endeared herself to the college students as counselor, confidante, and even at times matchmaker! In the seasons of fall and spring the news around the campus was that "Mrs. Hunt had office hours among her flowers on the lawn of the president's house." She was an avid supporter of the football and basketball teams and never missed a game, always seated in the front row of the cheering section. Old-timers recall with relish how Mary Ann acquired the habit of correcting the officials when they called certain plays about which she had a differing opinion. Hunt, as president of the college, deemed it inappropriate to sit with such a vocal partisan. He arranged with his chaplain, W. C. Mason, to sit with Mrs. Hunt while he sat with Mrs. Mason.

During their years at Emory and Henry College, Mary Ann graciously entertained the various distinguished speakers who came to the college, while at the same time she cared for her husband's aging and infirm mother. The college guests could have easily been accommodated at the historic and colorful Martha Washington Inn in Abingdon, but Mary Ann's critical and inquiring mind savored the after-breakfast and after-dinner conversations with the visiting intellectuals. In later years her husband remarked, "Mary Ann is the 'family liberal.'" During the episcopal years, she traveled with her husband on all of his overseas trips to England, Ireland, Sweden, Germany, Austria, Kenya, and Hawaii, and was a careful observer of the diversity of cultures, nationalities, and churches.

At ease in the role of wife of pastor, president, and bishop, Mary Ann knew her own mind and was a person of independent judgment. In the episcopal areas of Western North Carolina, Nashville, and Florida she became an active member of the local church—in Western North Carolina, Myers Park Church in Charlotte; in Tennessee, West End Church in Nashville; and in Florida, First Church in Lakeland. At the same time, in a quiet and gentle manner, she maintained her own individuality. Mrs. Rebecca Harmon, wife of Bishop Nolan B. Harmon, remarked approvingly, "Mary Ann is an independent soul, isn't she?" She was her own blend of supportiveness and independence.

In the meantime Hunt matriculated as a day student at East Tennessee State College in 1937. Four years later he received his baccalaureate with three majors (history, English, and education) and was valedictorian of the class. In college he distinguished himself in public speaking, winning regional and national honors in forensics, culminating in a diamond Pi Kappa Delta pin. The experience served him well during his seminary days when he coached the debate team at Emory University.

While Hunt was a student at East Tennessee State, he qualified as a local preacher and preached his first sermon after licensing in a little country church in Greene County, Tennessee. It was a frame building painted white, with a little steeple and a bell. Its dark pews were straight-backed and uncomfortable. Hunt recalls that it had "a pot-bellied stove in one corner and a much abused piano with a sound out of Tin Pan Alley in the other." The windows were an inexpensive variety of stained glass, and the hymnals had shaped notes. The choir was a group of men and women with more enthusiasm than musical talent. The congregation was made up of plain folk, most of them older, some shabbily dressed, and all bearing the visible marks of hard toil. It was summertime, and the profusion of new fans supplied by a nearby funeral home served as ready weapons against both heat and insects. Especially he remembers "the pulpit Bible . . . because the page on which [his] text would have appeared had been torn out, and [he] was compelled to begin the message with an unsuccessful appeal to memory."[11]

From his district superintendent Hunt received his first student-pastor appointment. The tiny little church known as College Heights was located just above the campus. Its members could not afford a preacher even as part of a circuit. The district superintendent asked Hunt to "go up there and preach" every Sunday. The salary for the entire year was forty dollars!

Something about his preaching did not appeal to the people at College Heights, and at the end of the year they requested that the district superintendent make a change. But that was not before the college student-pastor had spent the salary on a new suit of clothes.

Two years after the union of the three largest branches of American Methodism (Methodist Episcopal, Methodist Episcopal South, and Methodist Protestant) Hunt, the recent college graduate, packed his bags and headed for Atlanta to enter Candler School of Theology, Emory University. As late as 1941 the majority of candidates for the ordained ministry in The Methodist Church pursued the church's course of study route to ordination. In the Holston Conference the trend was already established that the normal route to ordination should be by way of a formal graduate theological degree, Bachelor of Divinity. The excitement engendered by four years of undergraduate education fueled Hunt's determination that he should follow in the path already being trodden by other Holstonians and go to seminary.

Candler School of Theology in 1941 was a relatively young institution. Southern Methodism historically had considered Vanderbilt to be its school, but in 1914 a rupture between university and church caused the southern church to consider founding new theological schools. As a result of this loss the southern church established two new universities: Emory in Atlanta and Southern Methodist in Dallas. Each had a theological school at the heart of the university: Candler at Emory and Perkins at Southern Methodist.

At the time of Hunt's entry Candler was beginning its twenty-sixth academic year. Within the short period of twenty-five years Candler had assembled a faculty of quality scholarship and experienced churchmanship. The fact that two of their early faculty were considered favorably in episcopal elections (twice W. Aiken Smart was almost elected, and Franklin Nutting Parker was elected but declined) attests to the school's standing in the broader church. Hunt reveled in the academic stimulation of Smart in New Testament, Parker in systematic theology (who had also served as dean), Henry Burton Trimble in homiletics (who succeeded Parker as dean), and Arva Colbert Floyd in missions. These professors stood out in the fledgling seminarian's mind. Two junior faculty members having recently arrived at Candler, William Ragsdale Cannon and Mack B. Stokes, became deep personal friends of Hunt even before they joined him as colleagues in the Council of Bishops.

At the outset of his last quarter at Candler, Hunt developed a persistent illness, diagnosed as infectious mononucleosis, which incapacitated him for periods of time and forced him to leave school. Dean Trimble secured permission for the ailing student to receive academic credit for a thesis (of dissertation proportions), which allowed him to finish the B.D. degree. The subject of the thesis, "The Evangelistic Message and Method of Dwight Lyman Moody," indicates that earlier formative influences of his youth now were coming into focus. Through the mediation of Moody's son, Dr. Paul D. Moody, one of the pastors of First Presbyterian Church in New York City, Hunt was able to have contact with some of the leading minds of the evangelical church of the day. They included Sherwood Eddy, G. Campbell Morgan, John R. Mott, Robert E. Speer, Henry Sloane Coffin, William Lyon Phelps, George C. Stebbins (hymn writer of such lyrics as "Have Thine Own Way" and "Take Time to Be Holy"), and his earlier acquaintance through the Youth Council, Dr. Howard Atwood Kelly, noted surgeon, Episcopalian layman, and one of the founders of Johns Hopkins University School of Medicine.

The Candler years were rich in personal relationships. A sizable contingency of Holston "sons" in the student body included Robert Lundy and his cousin, Gunnar Teilmann. Altogether the Holston roster tallied more than ten. They formed a circle of friendship that would extend across the years. Lundy, Teilmann, and Hunt formed particularly close friendships.

The Holston students, however, did not isolate themselves from the larger student body but embraced others from across the church, most notably the world church. Into this circle of comrades came a young Japanese student, Tatsumasa Shirakawa. A few days after the Japanese attack on Pearl Harbor, an agent of the Federal Bureau of Investigation arrested Tatsumasa (Ted) and held him at Fort McPherson. Dean Trimble was chief witness for the defense at Ted's trial and succeeded in persuading the authorities that Shirakawa was not a spy, but a sincere young man seeking training for the ministry. The young Japanese student was released as a ward of the dean and returned to his circle of friends, continuing to pursue his theological studies. From that circle of friendship, the core of which was Holston natives, Robert Lundy and Gunnar Teilmann would become missionaries in Malaysia. In 1964 Lundy was elected bishop of the Malaysian church, and he wrote the legislation requiring that thereafter a native of that part of the world would be the episcopal leader. Coincidentally, Lundy and Hunt were elected to the episcopacy the same year.[12]

Hunt's first-year student assignment was to the staff of First Methodist Church in Marietta, Georgia, where Dr. B. C. Gamble, a brother of Hunt's former pastor in Tennessee, was the senior pastor. At the conclusion of his first year of seminary studies, he was asked to become the pastor of the Sardis Church, in the Atlanta East District, between Powers Ferry and Roswell Roads. This appointment was to continue from June 1, 1942, until September 1, 1944. The Sardis Church traced its history to the War of 1812, the year of its founding. During Hunt's pastorate 276 persons were received into the membership of the church, most of whom came by baptism and/or profession of faith. A seminarian, Samuel A. Stanley Jr. from Virginia, and a local preacher, Harold Herndon, assisted him in his pastoral duties.[13]

A particularly sensitive issue arose in the Sardis Church, causing Hunt considerable concern. A couple in the church gave a beautiful crucifix to the church as a memorial and, obviously not understanding the difference between the plain cross and a crucifix, thought it should have a prominent place in the sanctuary. The matter was finally resolved by passing the crucifix to the church's youth fellowship to be used in their room. And a budding young pastor learned one of his first lessons in pastoral diplomacy.

Those acquainted with a dignified bishop with commanding posture and snow-white hair may find it difficult to learn that in his student days he was a prankster. His close Holston friends delight in telling about the pranks played upon classmates living in the old Dobbs Hall. His friends remember the late afternoon when he and Lundy went to dinner, leaving Teilmann in the shower. Hunt locked Teilmann's room door so that he could not reenter. Poor Teilmann was found later wrapped in a bath towel, dejectedly awaiting the return of his "friends." On another occasion, this time no prank but certainly an embarrassment to Hunt, late for a dinner appointment with Teilmann, Hunt charged down the steps of the Henry Grady Hotel in Atlanta, vaguely aware that a uniformed marine officer was coming up those same stairs. Hunt sideswiped the marine, and the young officer lost his balance and tumbled back to the floor level. Hunt offered profuse apologies as the marine dusted himself off and broke into a wide grin. "I accept your apology, young man, and you may tell your friends that you just did what no one but Jack Dempsey did before. You knocked down Gene Tunney!"[14]

Hunt's friend, Gunnar, joined the army as a chaplain in 1943 and was taken a prisoner of war in 1944. Prior to his capture in Normandy, he responded on April 12, 1944, from "somewhere in England" to a letter Hunt had written to him on February 15. In the initial letter apparently Hunt had made some inquiries regarding the chaplaincy. The struggle of conscience over military service when the country was engaged in critical combat was a very serious one for countless seminarians. Hunt had written to his bishop seeking advice about whether he should volunteer as a chaplain. Teilmann wrote his old friend:

> To be a chaplain in this man's army, one must be willing to have all his plans shot to pieces time and time again and not worry about it. . . . Now comes one of the things that will be hardest for you, taking orders from above. That's one thing on which you and I are just a little different. I don't mean that you can't take them, for certainly I know that you can, but sometimes they are so terribly absurd, that if I know Earl Hunt, he will rebel at some of them. . . . Earl, somebody has to stay there at home with the ideals that you and I have, and to my way of thinking those of you who have such a marvelous power in the pulpit ought to do it, and let us guys that are not so good at that, do our part by living in a simple way our religion here in the Army. . . . You need to be able to express your ideas powerfully, as you are able to do.[15]

A few years later Gunnar and his wife, Wava, joined Bob and Elizabeth Lundy in missionary service in Malaysia. While in Malaysia Gunnar suffered a serious heart attack. Now was Hunt's time to proffer pastoral advice to his longtime friend. The strength of the friendship between Hunt and his seminary classmate is revealed in a letter:

Please, old fellow, don't crowd your luck! While I don't actually believe your heart ever had time to have an occlusion, I do know that it happens in best of families! You never have had sense enough to take care of yourself, in which respect you have always resembled me uncomfortably, and I doubt that you have acquired any new sanity at this point. In other words, be good![16]

Another of Hunt's Holston friends was Harrison Marshall, who had gone to Perkins School of Theology in Dallas. When Marshall heard the news that Earl and Mary Ann were quartered in an apartment above the garage of Bishop and Mrs. Moore's home in Atlanta, he penned an epistle with pungent advice to Hunt: "I understand through an indirect source that you are borrowing a great many things from the Bishop, such as frying pans, china and silver. This is not so bad, but Hunt, please don't borrow any of his sermons as most of the people are familiar with them."[17] While Hunt was serious about his studies and his pastoral work, he did not forsake the bonds of friendship. Molded by the influence of family, church, and friends and equipped with a seminary degree, the young Hunt was ready to begin his itinerant pastoral ministry back in the hills of the Holston Conference.

Chapter Two

❧

Pastor

The Holston Annual Conference convened in Church Street Church, Knoxville, on October 11, 1944. Bishop Paul B. Kern, who had earlier ordained Earl Hunt as a deacon, was in the chair. On Friday morning a significant event in southern race relations had transpired. Three representatives of the African Methodist Episcopal Zion Church were introduced, including Bishop C. C. Alleyne, who spoke on better relations and understanding between the races. Three Holston pastors, Dr. J. W. Perry, Rev. Roy E. Early, and Dr. M. L. Gamble, were appointed to return the visit by attending the sessions of the annual conference of the A.M.E. Zion Church. For many present that day, it was a first. Dr. M. W. Boyd, president of Morristown College, an African American institution, followed with a presentation. After Dr. Boyd's presentation, a quartet of young women students from Morristown College sang "My Lord, What a Morning." Considering that there had been a tragic history, beginning with the separation of African American Methodists into three denominations and with the 1844–1845 split between the Methodist Episcopal and Methodist Episcopal South churches over the issue of slavery, it was quite "a morning!"[1]

Pastoral appointments were to be fixed at the adjourning session of the conference on Sunday. Consultation between the district superintendents, local pastoral relations committees, and pastors was a development yet to come for the church. Rumors abounded among pastors and laity regarding possible appointments, but the appointments would not be known until read by the bishop at the closing session. Rumors fed anticipation on the part of laypeople, but the same rumors generated apprehension and anxiety in many pastors.

The young, soon-to-be appointed pastor Hunt met his friend Bob Lundy in the hallway of the church.

"Bob, I'm so worried!" he exclaimed.

Lundy responded, "Earl, you were born worried! What is it now?"

"Rumor has it that one of us is to go to Broad Street Church in Kingsport to be associate pastor to Dr. Greer, and the other is to go to that strange new secret town, Oak Ridge, where there is no building and no parsonage and only a few members. I'd fall flat on my face if I were to go out there."[2]

On Sunday afternoon when the appointments were read, Lundy went to the new church development in Oak Ridge, and Hunt went to Broad Street Church as associate pastor. Apprehensions subsided, at least for the day. As it turned out, three newly ordained deacons were assigned to the Kingsport District that Sunday afternoon, and they became close friends. Ben St. Clair, fresh from Yale Divinity School, was appointed to West View Park; James Wilder, also a Yale graduate, went to Morrison Chapel and Litz Manor; and Earl Hunt went to Broad Street Church.

For one year Earl and Mary Ann made Kingsport their home and Broad Street their church. Dr. Robert E. Greer, the senior pastor, was terminally ill and died during the ensuing year. Hunt, the young neophyte pastor, had to shoulder responsibilities far beyond his years, and members of Broad Street Church readily commended him for his ministry during those difficult days.

Some members were so impressed with the young pastor's preaching abilities that they would have been quite satisfied to see him become Greer's successor. That was beyond the realm of possibility, however. After all Broad Street Church, measured by size and influence, was one of the four or five top churches in the conference. The Hunts knew full well that such an appointment was not possible, and they anticipated a change in appointment after just one year.

The annual conference sessions were held in Chattanooga in 1945 with Bishop Kern still the presiding officer. The appointments were read, and Hunt was assigned to Wesley Memorial Church in East Brainerd, a suburb of Chattanooga. Hunt was seated next to his friend Ben St. Clair when Bishop Kern announced the appointments.

Leaning over to his friend, he exclaimed, "Ben, I can't find this church listed in the statistical tables!"[3]

Sure enough, Wesley Memorial wasn't listed in the statistical tables. It did appear on the 1944 list of appointments, though. It was an infant congregation, birthed slightly more than a year before. An esteemed retired pastor, Dr. W. M. Morrell, had been the organizing pastor. No statistics! But soon Hunt was to discover one vital statistic. In Kingsport his salary had been $2,700. In the new Chattanooga appointment the salary was set at $1,300. Initially, the parsonage would have to be the guest room in the residence of his chairman of the board. Literally, the appointment was only a seventy-five-year-old farmhouse with a congregation whose membership was less than fifty.

During the five years of Hunt's pastorate at Wesley Memorial, the membership increased from 37 to 545. By the time his tenure was completed, the congregation had built a fine edifice valued in 1950 at $92,000, and a new parsonage had been purchased. Obviously in this case, congregation and pastor were admirably matched. What were the ingredients? In later years reflecting from a pastor's perspective, Hunt wrote:

> I have always believed that the pastoral ministry should have twin foci: the proclamation of the gospel and the care of God's people. Even when my homiletical knowledge was scant, I used to live literally for that shining moment when I would enter the pulpit to preach the Word. . . . But I have always been equally conscious of the opportunity afforded by purposeful pastoral visitation. In nearly a decade and a half of serving local churches, there was no year when I did not make at least two thousand pastoral calls. . . . I always knew from a source better than the lectionary, what would be a helpful homiletical menu for my people![4]

The Hunts brought his father and mother into their Chattanooga home to live with them in 1945. That was a pattern of life to be continued until Father Hunt's death in 1953, and until Mother Hunt became a nursing home patient in 1965. Over the years Mary Ann embraced Father and Mother Hunt with affectionate care. Church members often noted how she accomplished this ministry "without show."

In addition to these responsibilities, a new baby was born in the parsonage. On November 28, 1948, the Hunts' only child, Earl Stephen, was born. Steve completed his high school education in Charlotte in 1967 where his father was resident bishop. In 1971 he was graduated magna cum laude from Emory and Henry College and went on to earn a master's degree in international affairs from the American University in Washington and a doctorate with majors in political science and education from the University of Virginia. In Washington he met Edeltraut Gilgan from Hamburg, Germany, who was on the staff of the World Bank. The two were married in a bilingual service in the historic thirteenth-century St. Johannes Kirche in Eppendorf,

Hamburg, with Steve's mother in attendance and Steve's father assisting in the ceremony. Today Steve is the director for Planning and Policy and manager of International Programs, a unit of the U.S. Department of Education, and Edeltraut holds a responsible position with the Environmental Group of the Africa Region of the World Bank.

Earl Hunt's preaching ability was recognized widely throughout the conference. Two years in succession he was invited to be the preacher for the Enrichment Hour of the Holston Conference's annual Youth Assembly. Increasingly, invitations came to preach in local churches and district conferences. In 1950 he was appointed to First Church, Morristown, Tennessee. Although no one was surprised with the appointment, given the record of five years of spectacular growth at Wesley Memorial, it was nevertheless considered a jump in the usual appointment process. Conference members considered Morristown to be one of the four "second-tier" churches in size and influence in the conference. And he was only thirty-two years of age.

Morristown was to be home for the Hunts for the next six years. During those years, the membership of First Church swelled from 753 to 1,270. Quickly after arrival in Morristown, Hunt began to project a staff for First Church. He brought a young woman, Pat Rees, of Johnson City, to supervise the program of Christian education. Pat Rees was a graduate of Emory and Henry College and had served as the president of the Holston Conference Methodist Youth Fellowship. While on the staff at First Church, she met Gordon Cosby, who was nationally recognized as the founder of an exciting new experiment in church renewal known as Church of the Savior in Washington. Cosby brought Pat from First Church to be a member of his team at Church of the Savior. Reflecting upon her experiences working with Hunt at the Morristown church, Pat wrote:

Working with Earl has been the equivalent to master's work in seminary—he's taught me that much. And Mary Ann's concern and friendship have been part of a family I never had. The times I've never told Earl how much his sermons have meant and helped and the times I've failed to express proper gratitude to Mary Ann fairly haunt me but in a way, I felt it would have been saying the unnecessary to one's own family.[5]

In later years after marrying a Presbyterian pastor, O'Dell Smith, Pat still remembered how meticulous Hunt was, down to the last detail of the weekly Sunday bulletin.

The vision of great preaching that had sparked the days of his youth in the Johnson City Youth Council never departed from Hunt's sight. In the Wesley Memorial days he had brought to his newly established congregation members of the Candler School of Theology faculty along with Bishop Edwin Holt Hughes and Dr. John Stewart French. Now in Morristown the vision became even more ambitious. In November 1951 he brought Dr. James T. Cleland, professor of preaching and dean of the chapel at Duke University. Dr. Cleland was known as a dynamic Scottish preacher who had found a second home in America. People of other denominations quickly caught the spirit of the sponsoring congregation, and an ecumenical congregation packed the church.

On Friday evening the people of a county seat town in East Tennessee (some of the old-timers still remember) witnessed an ecumenical Eucharist. A Presbyterian minister celebrated the Sacrament of the Lord's Supper, assisted by a district superintendent, two pastors, and two superannuate ministers of The Methodist Church. Methodists, Baptists, Presbyterians, and Episcopalians communed together. The news of this ecumenical breakthrough appeared on the front page of the local newspaper.

Years later Hunt said, "I tried to bring great Christian voices into my pulpits in order that my people might have the inspiration that comes from hearing God's giants tell about their experiences of Jesus Christ."[6] And tell of their Christian experience they did! Speaking at these Spiritual Life Missions were some of the outstanding voices of the American church. In addition to Cleland, there were Bishop Ralph Spaulding Cushman, Bishop Paul B. Kern, Dr. Ralph W. Sockman, Dr. Albert P. Shirkey, Dr. Clovis G. Chappell, Dr. Clarence Edward Macartney, and Bishops (then Drs.) Cannon and Stokes. Noted laywomen were also on the list, including Mrs. Arthur J. Moore and Mrs. Catherine Marshall. Mrs. Marshall related to Pat Rees that the Morristown experience was her first experience on what would become an extensive speaking circuit. Frontline issues facing the church were represented by figures such as Gordon Cosby, whose bold new experiments in church renewal were being noticed widely, and Dr. John R. Mott, that indefatigable pioneer in ecumenism and the world mission of the church. Often in these popular annual services, Hunt called upon his friend Harold C. Harris, a prominent Holston pastor, and his wife, Marie, both proficient musicians, to lead the congregational singing and provide special music.

Dr. Mott was a relative of Lynn Sheeley, businessman and active member of First Church, and made annual visits to the Sheeley home. Mott spoke from the pulpit of the Morristown church every time he visited his relatives. Hunt recalls the first time Mott came to First Church during his pastorate. He noticed that Mott kept his head down and body bent low throughout the sermon. The preacher was not only curious but apprehensive. At the door of the church he met Dr. Mott and discovered that throughout the sermon he had been taking meticulous notes. The annual appearance at First Church of

John R. Mott, a Methodist layman with a vision of "the world for Christ in this generation" and Nobel laureate, was widely anticipated throughout the Morristown community. Each time he spoke at a service, the church was packed, and at his insistence the choir of Morristown College, the African American Methodist campus in Morristown, sang.[7]

First Church received thorough and frequent coverage of its developments in the local press. In 1952, after two years in Morristown, Hunt was voted Young Man of the Year. In the conference Hunt was increasingly recognized as one of the rising young leaders of the church. In 1955 he was elected third among the ministerial delegates to the General Conference of 1956. In the same year he was selected to be one of the preachers for the national radio broadcast called The Protestant Hour.

But other fields were beckoning. Hunt had already been made a member of the Board of Trustees of Emory and Henry College. In 1955 Dr. Foye Gibson, the president of the college, announced his intentions to resign to accept the presidency of Scarritt College in Nashville. In early February of 1956, Dr. Floyd B. Shelton, the chairperson of the joint Board of Trustees for Emory and Henry, Tennessee Wesleyan, and Hiwassee Colleges, visited with Earl Hunt in Morristown and indicated that the board's search committee wished to place Hunt's name before the entire board. Hunt was initially hesitant. He had from his seminary days committed himself to the pulpit and the pastoral ministry of the church. Hunt sought the advice of his bishop, Roy H. Short. He then wrote to Shelton:

> So fundamental is our sensitivity to the pastorate as the particular phase of the ministry to which God has called us that we simply cannot secure the consent of our own judgment to initiate a process which might take us away from it. If we could go to

Emory and Henry for a length of time comparable to a normal pastoral experience—say four to six years—and during such period make some helpful contribution to the College, then I think we might the more easily see our way clear to undertake such a ministry than is presently the case as we contemplate the Committee's understandable desire for a longer tenure.

Then the tone of the letter changed: "If, in the light of what I have written, your Committee and our Bishop feel that we should be drafted for this particular service, we would endeavor to follow the call of our Church wherever it should lead."[8]

The board of trustees lost no time. On February 21, 1956, the Special Nominating Committee presented its report, the essence of which was: "The Committee places in nomination Earl G. Hunt, Jr., for President of Emory and Henry College." With unanimous vote the board concurred. The college had just chosen its youngest president since 1836 when twenty-six-year-old Charles Collins had been summoned from Wesleyan University to be the school's first president. Hunt, a thirty-eight-year-old pastor, was to become the college's fourteenth president.

Chapter Three

❧

College President

"A little Oxford in the wilderness," an observer of academic institutions once described Emory and Henry College. The story of the founding of Emory and Henry College is an epic in Methodist annals. When the Holston Conference had but seventy traveling preachers and only 23,901 members, the undertaking was initiated. The conference itself had been organized just twelve years when the vision for a college captured the minds of the early Methodists.

When the conference met in Abingdon in the autumn of 1835, a committee was appointed to select a location for a college and manual labor school. The committee did not lose time. On January 1, 1836, the committee organized and proceeded to examine the proposed site, which is today Emory, Virginia. Named after Bishop John Emory, early Methodist bishop, and Patrick Henry, patriot and orator, the college's appellation expressed the guiding principles in the minds of the founders—Christian faith and public service.

The first students arrived on April 2, 1838, after the trustees had called Charles Collins, who was twenty-six years of age and a recent graduate of Wesleyan University in Connecticut, to be the first president. The enrollment for the first year, including preparatory and collegiate students, was one hundred. The school enjoyed steady growth until the clouds of war settled over the country in 1860. Two hundred eighteen students assembled for studies in 1860. No catalog was issued during the war period. The silence indicates that the students had answered the call of country.

Following the Civil War, the doors, behind which had been housed a military hospital during the conflict, opened again with the same number of students as enrolled in the initial year of the college. Financial support was always the major issue confronting the college's administration. There were no annual conference-apportioned funds for such an enterprise in the nineteenth century. The college managed to meet the financial challenges and continued to grow. New buildings were erected, new equipment was purchased, and new departments of instruction were established.

Even during the times of financial hardships, the college had staffed a scholarly faculty with strong commitments to the ideals of the institution and of its founding parent. But in 1941 war clouds again overshadowed the country, and the institution's existence was again threatened. A new president, Dr. Foye G. Gibson, arrived with uncanny fiscal and administrative abilities. The U.S. Navy selected Emory and Henry as one of the colleges and universities at which units of the navy V-12 training program were to be established. The first navy trainees arrived in June 1943. The work of the Emory and Henry Unit, which included the instruction of deck officer candidates, preaviation and pre-medical students, was highly commended by officials of the Navy Department. Following World War II, Dr. Gibson led the college into expansion of the physical facilities as the college increased its curriculum and faculty. Many people claimed that the administrative skills of Foye Gibson had saved the college.

Through years of hardship and years of growth, the college had attracted and sustained an enviable faculty. Some of its best-known faculty members commanded academic respect far beyond the little village of Emory. James Shannon Miller, a graduate of the University of Virginia and sometime student at the University of Göttingen, served as professor of mathematics for forty-nine years, and he was consulted on problems of higher math at home and abroad, especially in Germany. Fred C. Allison, a physicist who discovered two of the elements and the heavy isotope of hydrogen, was another noted faculty member. Allison was instrumental in bringing William Jennings Bryan, then secretary of state, to the campus to deliver a lecture, which was canceled due to heavy snow and subzero temperatures. However, through the solicitations of Allison, Bryan made a substantial contribution toward equipping the new physics building with a telescope, an instrument of which few small liberal arts colleges could boast.

The college counted among its graduates two governors of Virginia and one of Alabama. Confederate General "Jeb" Stuart was an alumnus, and Robert E. Humphreys (whose lab is displayed at the Smithsonian Institution in Washington), discoverer of the thermal process of cracking petroleum to make gasoline, had studied in the old halls of the college. Bishops Embree Hoss, James Atkins, and Walter Russell Lambuth had been students in the college. Before election to the episcopacy Hoss and Atkins had served terms as president of the college, as had Richard G. Waterhouse, who was elected to the episcopacy in 1910. One former president, Dr. J. Stewart French, was the chief author of the General Conference legislation uniting the three branches, Methodist Episcopal, Methodist Episcopal South, and Methodist Protestant churches, in 1939. Ranks of Holston Conference pastors and laypeople were proud graduates of the institution.[1]

While President Gibson's resignation was received with considerable regret, colleagues in the conference knew of his deep commitment to the mission work of the church. He had once served as a missionary in Poland. His decision to accept the presidency of Scarritt College was self-explanatory. Scarritt College was the church's primary center for the training and deployment of missionary personnel. With the announcement of the resignation, rumors circulated in the conference regarding the possible chances of Earl Hunt's appointment to the post. After all, Hunt had played a strong role in the recent capital funds drive to raise $1,750,000 for the three conference colleges: Emory and Henry, Tennessee Wesleyan, and Hiwassee. He was known among his colleague pastors as a "scholarly preacher." Throughout his life he had been a voracious reader. He was a student of history by way of biography. Already he was collecting a large biography collection of ecclesiastical leaders, theologians, and political figures. His hobby of autograph collecting had whetted his appetite for self-directed historical study. The community of Morristown knew him as "a cultured gentleman."

Other than as a student, Hunt had never acquired hands-on academic experience. Understandably, the distinguished history of the college and the records of its former presidents presented a daunting picture to anyone who might be mentioned for the post. Some in the conference were saying that the college was on the threshold of its greatest period. On the other hand, some voices were raised about the college's relationship with the church as this focused upon what was perceived to be a major campus "drinking problem." What the college needed in a leader was someone who would bring the college back into the fold of the church. The expectations for a new leader were indeed high, if not unattainable.

Hunt's hesitations were well placed. The demands were great. But for him what was even greater was the struggle of conscience over vocation. For years he had been confident that the divine call for him was to the pastoral and pulpit ministry of the church. At the time he wrote, "If I know my own heart my only ambition in the work of the Church and the Kingdom of God is to preach Jesus Christ." Therefore, he and Mary Ann "had always been wedded to the idea of service in a pastorate, and in this type of ministry we have been supremely happy."[2]

Two other pressures, in particular, weighed upon his conscience: "One was the extremely high value with which I assess the importance of Christian higher education in the total work of God's Kingdom today. The other was . . . that as a Methodist preacher I had no legitimate right to decline a call of my Church because of purely selfish interests."[3] He told the people of Morristown, "Mrs. Hunt and I will go to Emory at the proper time and will seek to make whatever contribution is possible to the College, to the church and to the Kingdom there."

The congregation of First Church experienced a poignant mixture of sadness and exhilaration. Some said that early in his ministry with them they had discerned "that Earl was destined for other things." They took pride in the fact that he was the only pastor they had ever had "who went on to become a college president."

In June the Hunts moved to Emory. With son Steve and Mother Hunt, they settled in the old antebellum president's house at the foot of the hill on the crest of which stood Wiley Hall, the college administration building. Quickly, Hunt assumed his new appointment and set to work.

Some in the college had wondered how Hunt would represent the college before the general public and a church constituency of pastors and laypersons. Some perceived his style to be quite formal, august, even at times pompous, and he could be emphatic, which raised suspicions that he would be rigid in his judgments.

Some staff members who accompanied him to speaking engagements in district conferences, pastors' meetings, and local church events discovered to their surprise that he had developed a standard presentation that he called his "cornbread and buttermilk" speech on the essentials of higher education. Observers noted from the outset that he could connect with the average church member in the pew and could do it convincingly. From the beginning he was building confident support from the grassroots of the church, crucial for the school.

Still some faculty members raised questions and verbalized intimations. There were some people, Professor George Stevenson related, "who were holding their breath when Earl Hunt arrived. They might not admit it now, but they had heard things and wondered just what he was going to do, especially after Foye Gibson. I couldn't imagine two persons more dissimilar than Foye and Earl."[4]

The "things" were no doubt related to several factors. Hunt had no earned doctoral degree (but neither had his predecessors). He was extraordinarily young for such a position (though the record had been set by the first president of the college). Then there was the persistent rumor that he had been sent to "dry up the college" (there was considerable agitation in the conference about this matter).

After eleven months in the office, inauguration day arrived, May 11, 1957. The campus was bursting with the foliage of late spring as the setting for colorful academic garbs and tradition-laden pomp and ceremony. Hunt particularly enjoyed the latter. Formal, celebrative occasions were a particular delight. The fourteenth president of the college was to be inaugurated.

Bishop Fred P. Corson, president of the General Board of Education of The Methodist Church, journeyed down from Philadelphia to represent the connectional church with a formal presentation. Bishop Roy S. Short, the resident bishop, came from Nashville to give the charge. Then the new president in an address announced his vision for the college.

He disarmed his audience at the start by quoting from the autobiography of the tenth president of the college, Charles C. Weaver: "I think the wisest move I ever made was when I decided to leave Emory and Henry."[5] The audience howled, and in the relaxed atmosphere the new president shared his vision that was to animate his administration.

With the illustration of Mark Hopkins sitting on one end of a log and James Garfield on the other, an illustration to which he would return repeatedly throughout his tenure, he emphasized, "A college exists to teach, and the ultimate measure of its contribution to human society is the effectiveness with which it does just that."[6] He then called the roll of some of the great teachers of the college. He had affirmed his faculty.

Then to the audience of the church he turned: "The church-related college ought to accept as one of its normal and fortunate responsibilities the training of professional and lay leadership for the Christian Church . . . nothing nebulous and apologetic will suffice."[7] The churches of the conference had waited to hear this.

Finally, his attention turned to the students and the college's responsibility in the formation of Christian character: "In a climate devoid of fanatical extremism and capable of reflecting with realism upon the problems of today's society, a sane, reasonable, and authentically spiritual presentation of the claims of Jesus Christ must be offered . . . to the delicate sensitivity of the mind and personality of modern youth."[8] He had tagged his bases; he had shared his vision. Seven years stretched before him.

Every administrator needs team players, and soon Hunt had

his. He had inherited a staff with strong loyalties to the college. Victor Armbrister had guided the academic program of the school since 1940 and was revered by faculty and students alike. Thomas L. ("Pidney") Porterfield, a local businessman, an active Presbyterian, and a former Emory and Henry football coach, had become the college treasurer and watchdog for the fiscal sanity of the institution. G. C. ("Connie") Culberson, an Emory and Henry alumnus, had been with the college for seven years working in alumni activities, student recruitment, fund-raising, development, public relations, and publications. He was the team's "utility player." W. C. Mason, another alumnus and a clergy member of the conference, was chaplain. "Chappie," as the students fondly called him, was an ardently loyal supporter of the new president. Hunt soon brought Fred Entler, city manager of Bristol, Virginia, to head the development office.

When in 1962 the beloved Dean Armbrister, who had been convalescing from an illness, suffered a fatal heart attack while attending a football game, Hunt had Armbrister's successor readily at hand. A protégé of Dean Armbrister, Daniel G. Leidig Jr. had completed his doctoral studies in humanities at Florida State University and had come to Emory and Henry to be a professor of English. Hunt swiftly convinced Leidig that he was the one to shoulder the mantle of the late dean. Hunt and Leidig were of equally commanding physical stature and shared their administrative responsibilities in a collegial fashion. Hunt's team was in place and remained so for the duration of his presidency.

Leidig considers Hunt's greatest contribution to the college to have been the academic developments that took form during his administration. Hunt's discipline of prodigious reading equipped him well to understand the academic needs across the curriculum. Immediately, he set himself to the task of improving the college's science laboratories. An isotopes laboratory and a language laboratory were provided for the Departments of Natural Science and Modern Languages, respectively.

Two endowed lectureships to augment the faculty's curricular contributions brought before the student body men and women in the religious, academic, literary, and political life of the nation. The Bays Blackwell Lectureship was inaugurated in 1962 by Sir Hugh Foot, then United Kingdom ambassador to the United Nations. The second, the Richard Joshua Reynolds Lectureship, was inaugurated in 1963 with Norman Cousins, editor of *Saturday Review,* as lecturer.

Curriculum was expanded, and additional faculty members were recruited. By 1963 the college could claim that fully 44 percent of the faculty had Ph.D. degrees. The curricular expansion required the full cooperation of dean and faculty. Under the leadership of Dean Leidig, the faculty undertook a major curriculum evaluation in preparation for the visitation of an accreditation committee of the Southern Association of Colleges and Universities in 1964.

The chair of the accreditation committee was Dr. Ellis Finger, president of Millsaps College, who with Hunt was elected to the episcopacy in 1964. Upon Finger's assignment to the Nashville Area, which included then the Holston Conference, Hunt remarked to his colleague, "Justice has been served. Now you have to implement the recommendations which your committee made to the college!"[9]

The Gibson administration had already begun a process of expansion of campus buildings when Hunt arrived. Hunt oversaw the completion of Martha Washington Hall, later to be called the Wiley-Jackson Hall, a large dormitory for women. The beautiful Georgian Memorial Chapel was completed with its spire looming over the campus. The Van Dyke Student Union was dedicated, and Hillman Hall, a new dormitory for men, was

erected. The Frederick T. Kelly estate of almost two million dollars permitted the beginning of a large, state-of-the-art library.
Also a new president's home, this time high on the hill, was nearly completed by the time Hunt left the presidency. Ralph
Sockman described the Emory and Henry landscape as the
"loveliest campus scene in academic America."[10]

The financial picture of the college improved both in operational budget and in endowment. By the end of Hunt's tenure
the college's budget allocated for faculty salaries showed a 120
percent increase. The operational budget had increased 145
percent, and the physical facilities had an increase of $2,750,000
in value. The gain in new assets for the last five years of his
administration was $1,143,478.39, or 21.5 percent growth. In
the period of 1960 to 1962, bequests amounting to at least
$1,750,000 came to the institution. During this same period,
Hunt was secretary of the executive committee of the Holston
Conference Colleges Development Program, which exceeded
its goal of $1,750,000 in pledges and cash for the capital
improvement of its three colleges—the exact amount that came
to Emory and Henry in bequests.[11]

In 1963 the students dedicated the student yearbook, *The
Sphinx*, to the president. The students' dedication read:

> To his family, he is a man of laughter and of love.
> To his colleagues, he represents intellect and integrity.
> To his community, he communicates the sense of vision and of
>   venture.
> To his church, he is a man with a mission and a message.[12]

Hunt soon learned that a college community is composed of
more than students and faculty. The support staff was indispensable and offered some of the most colorful personalities in the

campus community. Hunt may have projected an august and commanding presence, but he was no elitist. He cultivated close relationships with the college staff from secretaries to the buildings and grounds crew. In a tiny town like Emory it was easy for some members of the college maintenance staff to look upon him as mayor, town council, and local judge, all rolled into one. The events of one unusual evening illustrate this tendency.

On the Emory and Henry campus is a reflection pool, called the pond, fully supplied with swans and ducks. Past the midnight hour one evening, the nighttime watchman caught a male student, for reasons still undetermined, with two of the pond ducks, one under each arm. The night watchman, Joab Profitt, promptly marched the student to the door of the president's home and awakened the president in his pajamas, presenting him with a case of "theft" to be adjudicated, much to the student's embarrassment and the president's confoundment. Joab on the following day was overheard to say, "This college wouldn't be such a bad place if it wasn't for the students!" These were the night watchman's observations, not the president's.

From the Youth Council days in Johnson City, to the Spiritual Life Missions at First Church, Morristown, to the campus of Emory and Henry College, Hunt's admiration of great spokespersons of the Christian faith never diminished. Within one academic year such notables as Ralph W. Sockman, Charles Parlin, Brooks Hays, Elton Trueblood, Frank Laubach, and Norman Cousins spoke on the campus. Graduates of the college, promised Hunt, would not leave with a provincial understanding of religion and public responsibility. The convictions of faith were to be voiced by the most informed and eloquent proponents who could be found. The programs offered campus Christian apologetics in living form. What is known by only a few is that Hunt tithed the generous annual grant from the Holston

Conference, which went toward the financial undergirding of the religious speakers programs.

The civil rights movement that moved across the Southland underscored the questionable policy of the exclusion of African Americans from the student body of the college. Within the first year of his administration Hunt undertook informal discussions with Dean Armbrister and W. C. Mason about the possibilities of racial integration of the student body. Hunt has said in retrospect: "Integrating the College was part of my goal to make it a Christian college. I believe that Christianity doesn't have any meaning at all if it does not rise above race and culture and nationality and sex. I just didn't feel we were a Christian college until we were willing to accept qualified students regardless of race, culture, or creed."[13] At the very board meeting at which Hunt had been elected president a committee recommended "that the board of trustees continue to study the possibility of the admission of Negro students," and that "a special committee be appointed to study . . . and report its recommendations to the board."

The wheels of boards and committees grind slowly. For the board, some hard economic realities would carry considerable weight, even outcounting strong theological and moral arguments. The state of Virginia was at the time engaged in a massive resistance movement to prevent the racial integration of the public schools. The political and social climate of the state did not promise a favorable atmosphere. If the student body were to be racially integrated, it was estimated that the college could suffer a loss of $100,000 annually from its support constituency. The Virginia Foundation for Independent Colleges from which the school received annual grants was guarded about, if not resistant to, the idea. The foundation feared a backlash from its supporters if colleges benefiting from the foundation were to take such action.

In the summer of 1957, at the beginning of his second year, Hunt sent a carefully worded questionnaire to members of the faculty and other staff members to "determine their views on the subject" of integration of the college. The response was moderately favorable but not overwhelming by any means. Of the thirty-four replies received from the college faculty and administration, eighteen supported integrating the student body, ten agreed to abide by a board of trustees action whatever it might be, and six plainly disapproved. One faculty member declared that he would sever ties with the college if integration became a reality. Many of the thirty-four respondents favored delay or a time of proper preparations; six recommended that only black day students be admitted initially. Some faculty and administration persons stood firm in their religious convictions that by creation God had made no race inferior or superior to another. On the other hand, the specters of "social integration," "interracial dating," and "intermarriage" surfaced.

In the fall of 1957 the joint board of trustees of the conference colleges concluded that integration was "unwise from a practical standpoint." The report of the Coordinating Committee of the board allowed for continued consideration of the issue by observing that none of the conference colleges' charters contained a provision prohibiting admission of a student due to race. They therefore concluded that "the Executive Committee of each College" had "the authority to determine and execute a proper policy for that school on that matter."[14]

Hunt continued to pursue the issue of integration, even though a few board members had threatened his tenure if he integrated the college. On the preaching circuit within the conference, Hunt often commented on the Christian moral principle of racial equality. On the campus he encouraged his chaplain, W. C. Mason, to invite speakers who did not avoid the issue of racial integration. The president was attempting to create an atmosphere in which the moral objective of racial integration could be achieved with minimal conflict.

A campus poll was taken of the students, which indicated that they were almost equally divided on the issue. The majority, however, opposed integration. That the college years had a shaping influence on students' lives is probably seen in these results: the majority of students in the first- and second-year classes were overwhelmingly opposed, but a small majority in the third- and fourth-year classes favored such action.

Finally, the Executive Committee of the board in the fall of 1962 approved a policy permitting the admission of African American students. Committee members who played a positive role in changing the policy were Dr. R. R. Kramer, Dr. Charles C. Sherrod, retired president of East Tennessee State University, and Dr. Emmit Richardson, all laymen. Within the college Hunt had strong support for the policy from his dean, Daniel Leidig, and his chaplain, W. C. Mason. He knew he could rely upon strong support from key faculty members, and the climate within the student body was changing.

Initially, only African American day students were admitted. The pool from which such applicants could be cultivated was small. Only about 10 percent of the people in Washington County, in which the college was situated, were African American. One clergyman, a strong supporter of the college, wrote to the president expressing the hope that "the day will soon come when the restriction 'day' be omitted from the announced policy." President Hunt had addressed a letter to the parents of students. The father of one student answered Hunt's letter, stating "a sense of disappointment concerning the tone of the letter [from Hunt]. In the world we live in, I would have preferred a positive statement that neither race, creed nor color would be factors in admitting students to full participation in college life."[15]

The board's feared losses in revenue and students did not occur. The admissions office announced in 1963 a waiting list of students seeking entrance. The first African American student, Dorothy Hayes Brown, enrolled for two music classes with Dr. Charles Davis in the summer of 1963. Another local African American student enrolled for courses in the fall of 1963. They were not degree candidates, however. Hunt's tenure ended with his election to the episcopacy in July 1964. The cause continued through the leadership of Dean Leidig who, as acting president of the college, made a brief but passionate appeal to the board for full, unqualified integration of the campus. The board's chair, longtime supporter of the college, and former state senator William Neff immediately declared that he was in agreement with Leidig's appeal. The board swung in line behind the appeal, and a long struggle of approximately seven years ended. In later years Hunt regretted that the racial integration of Emory and Henry had not occurred much earlier. For him the issue had not even been debatable. It was the Christian thing to do.[16]

Since assuming the presidency in 1956, Hunt had with persuasiveness represented the college to its constituency. Internally, the college had grown in enrollment, financial support, and academic standing. He always chronicled these achievements with a degree of modesty and self-effacement. He credited his board, his faculty, and his staff with what had been accomplished. An indication of his modesty is reflected in a letter in 1978 to Edna Mae Scarborough, his diligent secretary through the years of his presidency:

> I remember the time I wrote a mean letter, and you typed it up beautifully and let me sign it. And then you tucked it away and

never mailed it. I have told this about a hundred times in sermons. It is probably only one of the many ways in which you kept
me from hanging myself across my presidential years and is representative of my many debts to you.[17]

The loyal secretary was seated with Mary Ann when Hunt was
elected to the episcopacy in 1964.

In the meantime the church was gearing up for the General
Conference of 1964 and, in particular, for the jurisdictional conference that would follow. The Southeastern Jurisdictional
Conference was to elect four new bishops. Bachman Gladstone
Hodge, elected in 1956, had been the last Holstonian to be
elected to the episcopacy. Now voices were to be heard in
Holston that Hunt's pastoral and presidential stature was such
that he should be considered for the episcopacy. Earlier several
inquiries by interested laypersons to their bishop asked if Hunt
could not be considered for appointment to the pulpits of their
churches. In both cases the churches were prominent ones in
the Holston and Tennessee Conferences. Hunt had been content to remain as president of the college. The rumors of a possible future for him were mounting. After all, he was known
across the Southeastern Jurisdiction as one of the most effective
preachers of the day. His record of administrative abilities was
widely known. Counter rumors floated within the jurisdiction.
In spite of his dignified and stately presence, he was too young.
What was more serious was the argument that by Southeastern
standards he was a social and political "liberal." At the sessions
of the annual conference in June 1963 he was elected to lead the
delegation to the General Conference. This action was tanta-
mount to an endorsement for episcopacy on the part of the conference.

Hunt knew of the rumors and so did the Emory and Henry
faculty. At the last faculty meeting of the 1963–1964 year he

made a statement to his faculty acknowledging the rumors, describing the current time to be ambiguous and uncertain. Nevertheless, he assured his faculty that he desired nothing more than to continue as their president but that, as always, he remained open to the leading of the Spirit and the call of his church.

Come July he would be among the four newly elected bishops of the Southeast. His affections for the college would continue, and his support of subsequent presidential administrations was enthusiastic and discreet. Once he left the presidency he had no intention of interjecting himself into the internal life of the college. In 1965 Emory and Henry College called him back to the campus to receive an honorary Doctor of Canon Law degree. The citation unmistakably bears the literary stamp of his former dean, Daniel Leidig, but the sentiments were those of the Emory and Henry family, both local and extended:

> Underlying his educational leadership has been the fundamental conviction that the Christian college must be the conscience of higher education in our time. As pastor and president he sought to unite faith and learning in vital relationship.

> At Emory and Henry he devoted his energies to the fulfillment of his dream of a great college. He built carefully and well. We are surrounded by the harvest of his concerns: his compassion in student and faculty relationships; the creation of a cultural program which exposed us to great minds of our time; the development of a superior program in the modern sciences; the quest for teachers possessed of both skill and purpose.

> He loved literature, and if he found less affinity for the barbaric yawp in language, he appropriated the more its felicity and its grace. His celebrated eloquence reveals a devotion to the Word, in its poetic as well as its prophetic dimensions.

In a difficult age he celebrates not man's mortality but his immortality, not the temporality but the transcendence of God. For eight years this voice summoned us on this campus not simply to be, but to become.[18]

❦

Chapter Four

Episcopacy

*T*he Holston Annual Conference met in Chattanooga in June 1964. The General Conference delegation headed by Earl Hunt had recently returned from the quadrennial sessions. The 1964 General Conference had been a highly significant one for several reasons. It was the last General Conference of The Methodist Church before the joining of The Evangelical United Brethren Church and the Methodists in 1968. A new United Methodist Church was on the horizon. In addition, throughout the 1950s and early 1960s the Methodists had been seeking ways to overcome the structural racial segregation of the church in the form of a Central Jurisdiction, which had been created in 1939. The Episcopal Address of 1964 had been explicit:

> We believe that this General Conference should insist upon the removal from its structure any mark of racial segregation and we should do it without wasting time.
>
> This will cost some Negro Methodists some of their minority rights. It will cost some white Methodists the pain of rooting out deep-seated and long-held convictions concerning race relations. But God Almighty is moving toward a world of interracial brotherhood so speedily and so irresistibly, that to hesitate is to fight against God and be crushed.[1]

That was the strongest statement against structural segregation in the church ever made by the Council of Bishops. The General Conference itself was of a mind that 1964 was the decisive year. Since 1956, legislation had existed permitting the transfer of African American local churches and conferences into the predominantly white regional jurisdictions. By 1964 there were still seventeen African American annual conferences. Pressure was building on both sides. Should the church enforce its resolution on race or wait until each geographical area of the country saw fit to take action? The conference placed a deadline of September 1967 when all African American annual conferences would be realigned according to the boundaries of the regional jurisdictions. The pressure of the conference's legislation was felt particularly in the Southeastern Jurisdiction where most of the resistance to the realignment existed.

As head of the Holston delegation, Hunt had the responsibility of giving the report of the General Conference to the entire body of the annual conference. The conference was not much affected by the proposal for a new United Methodist Church. After all, Evangelical United Brethren churches were hardly evident within the bounds of the conference.

The conference did feel the weight of new legislation with the final dismantling of the Central Jurisdiction. With his usual eloquence and sense of urgency Hunt told the conference that every church and every pew in The Methodist Church anywhere should be opened to African Americans. If a vote on the General Conference's legislation had been taken in Holston, most commentators are convinced that Holston would have strongly supported the General Conference's action. The conference did in 1968 proudly welcome the Southeastern Jurisdiction's first African American bishop, L. Scott Allen, as its new bishop. The secular press in Chattanooga, however, the morning after Hunt's address carried an account of the previous evening's session with a headline reading "Hunt Favors Mixing." The press report was to surface later at the jurisdictional conference. In the meantime Holston's delegation to the July meeting of the Southeastern Jurisdiction was solidly behind Hunt for election to the episcopacy.

The jurisdictional conference convened at Lake Junaluska, North Carolina, on July 8 and received the recommendation of the Committee on Episcopacy that with the creation of a new Raleigh Area the conference should set itself to the task of electing four new bishops. The balloting began. On the second ballot W. Kenneth Goodson, senior pastor of the large Centenary Church in Winston-Salem, was elected. On the seventh ballot Edward J. Pendergrass, senior pastor of an equally large church, First Church, Orlando, Florida, was elected. Beyond the seventh ballot the conference proceeded slowly. The leading contenders were H. Ellis Finger Jr. of the North Mississippi Conference, William R. Cannon of the North Georgia Conference, and Earl G. Hunt Jr. of the Holston Conference. Coincidentally, all three were known educators. Finger was president of Millsaps College in Jackson, Cannon had become dean of Candler School of Theology at Emory University, and Hunt was president of Emory and Henry College.

On the thirteenth ballot Finger was elected, and Hunt's support had almost disappeared, falling from a high of 122 votes on the third ballot to only 37 votes on the fourteenth and fifteenth. Cannon led through ballot twenty-one. Carl J. Sanders of Virginia withdrew but would be elected at the 1972 conference. Hunt was ready to withdraw also, but two lay delegates in the Holston delegation, Dr. Charles C. Sherrod and Dr. Russell R. Kramer, both trustees of Emory and Henry College, urgently persuaded him to refrain from doing so. Edgar A. Eldridge, a

Holston clergy delegate and a teller who had been watching the configuration of votes, informed the delegation that Hunt was "moving up" from 37 votes on the fourteenth and fifteenth ballots to 60 votes on the eighteenth. "We knew that Earl was going to be a bishop," says Eldridge. "We simply did not know when."[2]

On the twenty-second ballot Hunt pulled into the lead and was elected on the twenty-fourth ballot. Dean Cannon, who had been leading until the twenty-second ballot, ever the gracious southerner, rose on the floor and stated how proud he was that his former student had been accorded this recognition by the church. Cannon, who was known for his photographic memory, had momentarily suffered a lapse of memory. Although he was a junior faculty member at Candler when Hunt was a seminary student, he had never been Hunt's professor.

Hunt's gracious spirit prevented him from ever correcting Cannon's memory. In 1997, shortly before he died, Cannon completed his autobiography still "remembering" that he had been Hunt's seminary professor. Hunt confesses that he and other seminarians at Candler avoided Cannon's courses. Cannon had come to Candler after having received his doctorate from Yale with the highest of academic honors. Only a one-year pastoral appointment at Oxford, Georgia, had separated his Yale experience and his beginnings as an academic on the Candler faculty. The rumor in the student body was that Cannon gave his students unusually low marks. Hunt and others were fearful that a sojourn in a Cannon course could drastically affect their point average.[3]

Nevertheless, Cannon's tribute was a poignant moment in the conference, and he and Hunt continued to be close friends until Cannon's death. Hunt authored the foreword to Cannon's autobiography and reflected that "across the long future years the pendulum of the Cannon perspective appeared to swing to the opposite extreme as he again and again lavished huge amounts of extravagant praise upon many of us whose ordinariness could never justify such adulation."

Bishop Roy Short commented on this moment in the jurisdictional conference when a seminary dean paid a moving tribute to a younger colleague in ministry:

> Bishop Cannon's emotions run deep, and he does not hesitate to express them by a warm embrace. A beautiful example of this came in 1964 at the Southeastern Jurisdictional Conference. . . . When the chair announced the election of Dr. Hunt, Dr. Cannon literally ran across the auditorium and heartily embraced the pupil who had been elected over him.[4]

One historical note seemed to escape everyone's attention. Hunt was the only minister with natal roots in the former Methodist Episcopal Church to become a bishop in the Southeastern Jurisdiction of The Methodist Church. By 1964 this simply didn't matter. The divided church of pre-1939 days no longer prevailed. Another historical note should be recorded. When only one bishop was chosen four years later, in 1968, it was Cannon who was elected–and it was on the twenty-fourth ballot!

In 1987 Hunt surveyed the election process for bishops. In the interim between 1964 and 1987 the General Conference had formulated a process whereby candidates could be officially nominated by their annual conferences. Hunt regarded this as a further politicizing of the process. He wrote:

> I am opposed to the present method being used in our Jurisdictional Conferences to elect men and women to the episcopacy. It politicizes the process in a way that can easily prevent

a superior but unsponsored person from being chosen. It enables the larger Annual Conferences to pool their votes by previous agreement and so control ballots, thus virtually eliminating the equally important chances of smaller Conferences to promote able and worthy prospects. If the procedure of asking "candidates" to appear before delegations for statement and subsequent interrogation is employed, it tends to diminish the dignity and perhaps even to compromise the integrity of these men and women. . . . I belong to a generation that at its best believed the office should seek the person, and not the person the office; and to a vanishing company of bishops who were elected in a manner that may not have been entirely pure but one that had not reached the level of political maneuvering we know today.[5]

Bishop Hunt did not note, however, that the process he critically examined had been hailed as one that would bring episcopal elections "out of the back room" and into open, public scrutiny. Still, to onlookers as well as many participants, either process seemed to foster less than adequate Christian discernment. Judge Tom Matheny, a longtime member of the Judicial Council of the church, called for a changing of the atmosphere "of the whole process" from the election of delegates to the conduct of jurisdictional conferences.[6]

Hunt's perspective on the episcopacy was succinctly stated in a book he authored in 1980: "I have tried to remember across recent years that I am first of all a Christian, then an ordained minister of the gospel, and finally a bishop of the church—and I mention these identities in what I regard as a descending order of importance."[7] In bidding farewell to the Western North Carolina Conference in 1976, he expressed the same sentiments:

I have never had any delusions about this job which the Church gave me now nearly twelve years ago. I have always had immense respect for it, but I have never felt that election to the episcopacy gave an individual a right to think of himself as a "bishop of the church." I have felt that somehow that right, if ever it should come, would come as a result of dedicated service in that office of the ministry as in any other.[8]

Upon his election and its announcement in the press, two revealing communiqués arrived. One came from Ralph W. Sockman, who had just retired from a distinguished pastorate at Christ Church in New York City:

Dear Earl:

Heartiest congratulations on the new office. I have not heard where you are to be assigned, but I know wherever you go you will render great service.

As I recall it, I wagered $1,000 that you would be elected.

Will you refresh my mind on this point, and payments may start at your own convenience.

From an old friend in the Southeastern Jurisdiction who had preached for Hunt on many occasions came the following telegram:

Dear "Big Earl":

Your election to the episcopacy has not caused me to revise my opinion of that office, but it has made it more difficult for me to say about it what I have been saying! Congratulations!

Clovis Chappell[9]

Charlotte Area, 1964–1976

When the Committee on Episcopacy issued its assignment report, Hunt was placed in the Charlotte Area, which is comprised of the Western North Carolina Conference, one of the largest conferences in the connection. Hunt was forty-five years of age. His predecessor in the Charlotte Area was the venerable Nolan B. Harmon Jr. Bishop Harmon had been the book editor of The United Methodist Publishing House and was widely recognized as the leading scholar on United Methodist polity and related constitutional issues. Hunt, the youngest bishop in the Southeastern College of Bishops, was to follow Harmon, who by many was regarded to be the sage of the church.

The job of bishop demanded maturity of judgment. The church had not waited for Hunt to have the years required for many to gain such maturity. The church expected that maturity immediately! A mark of his mature leadership is seen in that when he had served the *Disclipline's* limit of two quadrennia, the Western North Carolina Conference requested the jurisdictional conference to vote for an exception to the limit of two quadrennia and return Hunt to the Charlotte Area. The jurisdictional conference complied with the request. Hunt returned to Charlotte for an additional four years.

A Western North Carolina pastor, John James Miller, relates an amusing story revealing the new bishop's rather humble understanding of his office. Dr. Robert G. Tuttle, Sr., was leading evangelistic services at First Church, Dallas, where Miller was the host pastor. One night after services, Miller missed his eight-year-old son, Perry, and learned that the young boy had answered the call to Christian commitment and was meeting with the evangelist in the inquiry room.

Sometime later at a district dinner meeting where Bishop

Hunt had been invited as a special guest, young Perry arrived late with his family and sat at the only available seat which was next to Bishop Hunt. During the course of the meal Perry looked up at the Bishop and declared, "I have given my life to Christ."

Hunt answered, "Very fine."

Perry's rejoinder was, "I want to tell you about it," and Hunt listened intently to the young man as he told of his experience in detail.

Then he asked the bishop, "Have you ever committed your life to Christ? Tell me all about it. Who was preaching and did he invite you to come forward?" The Bishop related in detail to the persistent lad his own conversion experience back in Johnson City, Tennessee, years ago in his youth.[10]

Upon arrival in Charlotte, the new bishop immediately set himself to the task of overseeing the reorganizational pattern of the Western North Carolina Conference to conform to the Conference Program Council concept. He appointed Dr. C. C. Herbert, the area's first administrative assistant to the bishop. Later Dr. Charles D. White would assume these responsibilities. Herbert and White rendered the bishop able administrative assistance in the organizational work of the conference. To coordinate the work of the conference's five colleges—Brevard, Greensboro, High Point, Pfeiffer, and Bennett—he set in place a College Coordinating Council with an executive secretary, a plan somewhat similar to what he had experienced as a college president in the Holston Conference.

The proclamation of the gospel was always central in the bishop's ecclesiology. The vision of great preaching that had gripped him in his youth in Johnson City never left him, so he had a vision for his new episcopal area. He had a dream for an Institute for Homiletical Studies.

On a snowy February day in 1965 over snow and ice he journeyed to Thomasville, North Carolina, to keep an engagement with Mr. and Mrs. George D. Finch. At the conclusion of an afternoon conversation with the Finches, the bishop was assured of their enthusiastic and generous support to underwrite the new experiment. The Finches agreed with their bishop's Scripture-based inquiry, "How shall they hear without a preacher?"

To supervise the planning and initiation of the new Institute for Homiletical Studies, Hunt appointed Cecil Heckard, district superintendent of the Gastonia District, and Wilson Weldon, pastor of the West Market Street Church in Greensboro. Weldon would shortly thereafter move to Nashville to assume new responsibilities as editor of The Upper Room. The Western North Carolina Conference elected a board of trustees consisting of one member of the Conference Board of the Ministry, one member of the Conference Board of the Laity, one clerical member of the Conference Board of Evangelism, one clerical member of the Conference Commission on Town and Country Work, one clerical member of the Conference Board of Education, one layperson from each district, four cabinet members, one representative of the Duke Endowment Rural Church Program, two representatives of Duke Divinity School, and the president of the Conference Coordinating Council. Such distributed representation assured that the new project had the full support of the widest constituency of the conference.

By 1966 the various components of the institute were in place, and the new program was inaugurated. Structurally, the plan called for five programmatic parts. First was the Clinic in Preaching, designed for pastors who served as lay pastors, associate members, and full members of the conference who were not seminary graduates. The clinic was comprised of six four-hour sessions. Over the first six years of the institute's life the clinic averaged an enrollment of thirty-two pastors, and over this period nearly two hundred pastors were involved in this sector of the institute's program. The sessions of the clinics were held on the campus of Duke Divinity School with Dr. Thor Hall, professor of preaching at Duke, as the principal lecturer. Looking back upon the experience, one of the pastors wrote that it "was probably the most useful experience in my entire ministry. . . . Thank you for helping to make a better preacher out of this 'poor hillbilly boy.'"[11]

The second feature of the institute consisted of the Bishop's Dialogue with Young Ministers. The objective was to provide an occasion for the bishop to engage in intensive conversation with probationers and full conference members who had six or less years of service and who were currently serving pastorates. The plan projected four dialogue sessions annually, located at strategic geographical spots. The young pastors were quite responsive with 112 attending dialogues in the first year. The success of the first year prompted the committee to project new groups of pastors for future years—first, pastors with eight to sixteen years of service; second, pastors with nine to nineteen years of service; and third, pastors with twenty or more years of service. In any single year approximately three hundred pastors were engaged in the dialogue sessions. The sessions did not focus solely on preaching. Wilson Weldon has commented that topics ranged from "ministerial salaries to COCU, from the appointment-making process to existentialism, from ministerial ethics to the Jesus movement, from social activism to individual pietism, from glossolalia to hermeneutics."[12] With the social and political turbulence of the 1960s, the ferment that permeated the society, and the pangs of generational transition in both society and church, these dialogue sessions provided the opportunity for bishop and pastor in face-to-face contact to become more knowledgeably engaged with the critical issues confronting church and society.

The third sector of the institute was the Bishop's Reading Program. A panel of consultants chosen from the Western North Carolina Conference was asked to submit entries for a reading list of the most important books on preaching, theological, and biblical studies. A revised reading list was prepared each year, and every pastor serving an appointment received a loose-leaf notebook for record keeping of the pastor's reading program. Each new pastor received an Award Book when the pastor was admitted on trial. In addition, the new pastor received a new book each year for three years, upon certification that three books on the recommended reading list had been read during the year. Dr. Thor Hall of Duke Divinity School chaired this aspect of the program in the early years.

The fourth aspect of the program was the annual Award Sermon Challenge in which probationers and members of the conference having six years or less of effective service submitted each year one of the sermons preached to their congregations. An award was made annually to the pastor preaching the best sermon in his or her district. From these sermons a selection was made of the three best sermons preached in the conference for that year. On the annual conference level the pastor presenting the best sermon of the year preached before the sessions of the annual conference and received either a $250 book award or a scholarship to attend one of the special study programs at a theological school. Among the best sermon award recipients was J. Lawrence McCleskey, who was elected to the episcopacy in 1996.

The feature of the institute receiving the most recognition and attention was the annual series of Lectures on Preaching. The Finches assumed full financial support of this segment of the

institute and provided the means whereby some of the most outstanding preachers from North America and across the world
would come to the Western North Carolina Conference. The
opening series featured the famed New Testament scholar and
preacher Dr. James S. Stewart of Edinburgh, Scotland. In following years the lecturers included Bishop Francis Gerald
Ensley, then resident bishop of the Columbus (Ohio) Area; Dr.
Bryant M. Kirkland, pastor of Fifth Avenue Presbyterian
Church in New York City; Dr. A. Leonard Griffith of Toronto,
Canada; Dr. Leighton Ford of the Billy Graham evangelistic
organization; Dr. Robert E. Goodrich Jr. of Dallas, Texas, and
later to become a bishop; and Dr. R. Leonard Small of St.
Cuthbert's Church, Edinburgh, Scotland. In 1972 the
Homiletical Institute published a volume including sermons
preached by the first six lecturers. Some observers have concluded that rarely on the American scene have the great
Christian preachers of the day been assembled in a continuing
program such as in this lecture series. Certainly, the "pulpit
greats" brought renewed attention to the "lively Word" as they
preached in Charlotte and High Point.[13]

If pastors and their preaching ministry were in the forefront
of the newly arrived bishop's objectives, equally so was the bishop's concern that the voice of the laity be heard. Early on he
undertook the task of organizing a Lay Advisory Council to meet
at regular intervals to hear the bishop interpret current issues
before the church, and in turn the forum provided the bishop
with an opportunity to hear representative lay voices and perspectives from across the conference. Most conferences of the
church did not have a regularly scheduled and systematically
ordered forum for the lay voice. Some pastors felt that the bishop was listening too much to the laity, when for years many
laypersons had been convinced that bishops listened primarily to

the voices of the clergy. Whatever tensions may have existed between the two, judgments appear to have been resolved when in 1985 the Western North Carolina Conference unanimously voted to make Hunt an honorary member of the conference, nine years after he left the Charlotte Area. The resolution adopted by the conference in part read: "He brought . . . graciousness and concern to every pastoral contact, and unprecedented relationships with the laity."[14]

Hunt's vision of forums where the voices of clergy and laypersons could be heard directly by their bishop was actualized in these two structures: the Institute for Homiletical Studies and the Lay Advisory Council. This vision would persist in future episcopal areas where he served.

Squarely before the Southeastern annual conferences was the action of the 1964 General Conference regarding the merger of Central Jurisdictional conferences with the regional jurisdictions and conferences. For the Southeastern conferences this was not just a matter of implementation of juridical polity. This was profoundly a moral question, since it called for the racial integration of the church, at least on the structural level of annual conferences. The 1964 General Conference's legislation was made imperative when in 1968 the union of the former Methodist and former Evangelical United Brethren churches was effected. The structured segregation of the church by means of the Central Jurisdiction simply ceased to exist. The Evangelical United Brethren wanted no part in a church where such a structure existed.

This issue of a structurally segregated church had been a major sticking point in the merger negotiations. In the called sessions of the General Conferences of the two churches in 1966 the matter was finally settled. The former Methodists had no later than 1972 to eliminate all forms of the Central Jurisdiction.

Hence the Plan of Union of 1968 closed the chapter of the former Methodist Church's racially structured jurisdiction. No such structure was in the Plan of Union. One observer remarked that structured segregation on the level of conferences ceased with "an eloquent silence."

Approaching the 1968 annual conference sessions, the Western North Carolina Conference knew that the time of definitive decision was at hand. The conference had begun the deliberations with resolutions in 1965, 1966, and 1967. Over these years, Hunt had worked with his cabinet and Lay Advisory Council in preparing for the merger of the overlying districts and churches of the North Carolina-Virginia Annual Conference of the Central Jurisdiction with the Western North Carolina Conference. He had forthrightly told his cabinet that when such a decision was implemented, he intended to appoint an African American district superintendent. The role of the Lay Advisory Council was critical. The persons on the council had persuasive voices that influenced members of local churches.

In one session of the Lay Advisory Council, after hours of struggle between emotion and reason, George Ivey, a prominent businessman with a chain of department stores throughout the South, spoke, "It will surprise all of you for me to make this motion. But I have heard our bishop lay this matter upon our Christian consciences, as have you, and now I move that our informal body give him a unanimous vote of confidence as he carries out his announced plan, and that we reinforce that vote by returning to our communities and our districts helping our neighbors and friends understand and accept what is happening."[15] On that Saturday afternoon in Charlotte, this action of the Lay Advisory Council constituted a major step toward the success of any subsequent action. Tensions did arise in some quarters of the conference. To some, it seemed that the bishop was being "pushy." Hunt nevertheless persisted.

The annual conference of 1968 received the final resolution for merger with the North Carolina-Virginia Conference districts and churches and with an overwhelming vote passed the resolution. Statistically, the North Carolina-Virginia Conference overlay with the Western North Carolina Conference consisted of 2 districts, 109 churches, 61 pastoral charges, 35 effective clergy, and 10,917 members. When the resolution for merger was adopted, Hunt clearly reminded the full conference of his earlier statements that at the proper time, after implementation had taken place, he would carry through with his promise to appoint an African American district superintendent, which meant that the number of districts would be expanded from 13 to 14.

Following the conference's action in a symbolic moment, Bishop Hunt and Bishop Edgar A. Love of the Central Jurisdiction jointly read this statement: "For the glory of God and for the extension of Christ's Kingdom in our time, we announce officially the merger of the Western North Carolina Conference of The United Methodist Church with that portion of the North Carolina-Virginia Conference lying within its borders. May our Heavenly Father abundantly bless this union. Amen." Representatives of each of the conferences, the Reverend J. Clay Madison and Mr. Richard Erwin, now a federal judge, made appropriate responses. Bishop Love then spoke at the preaching hour on the subject "A New Relationship— Friends."[16]

The record is clear that the Western North Carolina Conference had acted with an overwhelming vote of Christian conscience. In 1965 the vote for merger had been 958 for and 45 opposed. In 1966 the same pattern had prevailed, 761 for and 58 opposed. In 1967 again the same pattern continued with 849 for and 60 opposed. The 1968 vote was predictable. In matters of race relations the conference was one of the more progressive conferences of the jurisdiction.

One figure in particular stands out. Julian A. Lindsey had been in the cabinet for only one year, and he worked with determination with his bishop to effect a plan whereby his district, Winston-Salem, would be divided into two districts, providing a district for the appointment of the African American district superintendent. The cabinet was not of one mind, but Lindsey and Hunt persevered.

The result was the formation of two districts from the old Winston-Salem District: the Winston-Salem-Northeast District and the Winston-Salem-Forsyth District. The twenty-five pastoral charges in the city of Winston-Salem along with ten charges in adjacent Forsyth County would be the more urban district, and to this district should be appointed the new district superintendent. The so-called Northeast District was completely outside the city limits of Winston-Salem and extended from Mount Airy on the west to Reidsville on the east and included the area on both sides of Pilot Mountain. Lindsey would be the superintendent of this district, the character of which was more small town and rural. Lindsey recalls that among others, three pastors in Winston-Salem were quite supportive of the change: Ernest A. Fitzgerald of Centenary Church; Orion Hutchinson Jr. of Ardmore; and H. Claude Young Jr. of Maple Springs. In 1984 Fitzgerald would be elected to the episcopacy.

Dr. James C. Peters was appointed to the Winston-Salem-Forsyth District and became the first African American in the Southeastern Jurisdiction to be appointed a district superintendent and superintendent of a district composed of a large majority of white churches and pastors. In 1974 Hunt appointed

Cecil H. Marcellus Jr., another African American pastor, to the superintendency of the Northeast District. The merged conference celebrated the merger with commitment to a new day in the life of the church.

Dissonant voices, to be sure, were raised in some quarters of the population. Whether they were, for the most part, United Methodist voices, the record is not clear. Hunt does report that, on four occasions, persons purporting to be members of the Ku Klux Klan threatened his life and the lives of his family members. Following a worship service in Matthews, North Carolina, Hunt relates that the visiting evangelist came to him to report a conversation with a new convert who had told him that the Hunt family had been targeted for an attack (a bomb was to be thrown into their house) on a weekend when the bishop would be in residence. The new convert claimed to know this because he professed to have been the Klan member charged with this duty. Whether the threats had any real substance would have been difficult to ascertain. Hunt hired at his own expense for two years a person to stay at the episcopal residence with his wife and son when he was on the road. In any event no threat ever materialized, and matters settled down.[17]

In an article in the *Charlotte Observer*, July 27, 1972, as Hunt began his final four years as bishop of the Charlotte Area, he was quoted as saying, "I want to see a maturation of our merger with the former North Carolina-Virginia Conference."[18] Minority persons were appointed to the conference program ministries staff, and the bishop continued to call the church to "settle down to the nitty-gritty processes of working together as Christian men and women in building a great Christian Church without regard to race."[19] By 1972 approximately sixty congregations in the conference could claim to be at least partially integrated, which was out of a total of approximately twelve hundred churches in the conference. Hunt, however, saw that integration was a two-way matter. In 1973 he was calling upon the conference and members of local churches with this message:

> White members in many of our communities should consider uniting with predominantly black churches, so that membership movement may be in both directions. . . . For practicing Christians, the solution of problems related to race is still disturbingly simple: It lies, as I see it, in the sincere and honest posing of a very old question—What would Jesus Christ have me, His follower, to do?[20]

Hunt's years in Charlotte were years of ecumenical growth. The church's complicity with the larger society in racial segregation, Hunt's analytical mind told him, was compounded by its internal division between Catholics and Protestants. Shortly after arriving in Charlotte, he became acquainted with Bishop Michael J. Begley of the Roman Catholic Diocese of Charlotte. Begley was a jovial, warmhearted Irishman who embodied the spirit of Vatican II. Soon he and Hunt became close friends. For six Christmas Eves Bishops Begley and Hunt went as an ecumenical team to the Mecklenburg County Jail to visit and pray with the prisoners. Annually, they exchanged pulpits with Begley preaching at First United Methodist and Hunt at St. Patrick's Cathedral. Together they sponsored a week-long institute for United Methodist and Roman Catholic clergy featuring Archbishop Fulton J. Sheen.

On November 21, 1973, Hunt addressed an ecumenical luncheon cosponsored by the two bishops. In one of the most scholarly, yet affectionate, addresses of his episcopacy, Hunt drew upon the Methodist legacy of John Wesley's sermon "The Catholic Spirit," together with his *Letter to a Roman Catholic,* and the dialogues between the Roman Catholic Church and the World Methodist Council. In particular, though, he invoked the spirit and influence of "that remarkable Christian man," John XXIII. From the outset Hunt's address faced squarely one of the most difficult and perplexing issues in ecumenical relations, namely, authority in the church. He proceeded to relate other issues (ministry, sacramental practice, order, and ordination) integrally to the issue of authority. He clearly demonstrated within a short time that he knew precisely where the tough issues were, and he knew how to delineate the thorny theological issues in a way understandable by lay and clergy, Catholic and Methodist alike. Concluding the address with a typical Hunt illustration drawn from biography, he drove home the unmistakable import of the ecumenical gathering:

> Years ago I heard the celebrated Anglican missionary, the late Sir Wilfred T. Grenfell, tell an amusing but haunting story. . . . He had returned from his medical work in Labrador to make a speaking tour through Canadian and American cities for the purpose of raising funds to carry on his labors. In a certain church in Seattle, Washington, Dr. Grenfell chanced to tell the story of a native woman in Labrador whose leg had had to be amputated and who desperately needed an artificial limb. At the close of the message, a woman came forward and told Dr. Grenfell that she would bring to his hotel the next morning an artificial limb which had belonged to her deceased husband, with the hope that he would accept it as her gift for his Labrador patient. In relating this occurrence, the famous missionary concluded with this telling sentence: "When I, an Episcopalian, took from this Presbyterian woman an artificial limb which had belonged to her Methodist husband and which she had promised to me as a result of a sermon delivered in a Baptist church, my Roman Catholic

friend in Labrador could walk again!" This is the spirit of Christ at work in an ecumenical setting to bring healing to the hurt of the world. And this, surely, is the exalted mood of today's luncheon fellowship and the high and holy resolve of all of us as we set our faces toward the future.[21]

In 1989, the Diocese of Charlotte celebrated the twenty-fifth anniversary of its founding. The diocese's beloved founding bishop, now eighty-seven years old, was given special recognition. Bishop Hunt was an invited guest-participant in the festivities seeking to fulfill an ecumenical hope and commitment of earlier years:

> There is, perhaps, but a bare beginning of that ultimate understanding between our two communions which can result in a blessed Christian reunion. But let us rejoice that the beginning has come, and let us permit ourselves in glad amazement to note the rapidity with which changes in attitude and feeling have developed in little more than a decade of time.[22]

One of Hunt's prized memories of the Charlotte period is the honorary Doctor of Humane Letters degree conferred on him by the Benedictine Belmont Abbey College.

Three major concerns of Hunt's episcopacy over twenty-four years concisely summarize the first twelve years, the Charlotte years, of his tenure. The art of preaching was his persistent priority for the pastors, but for the areas of his episcopal leadership he consistently lifted up *learning, evangelism,* and *social responsibility.* In the area of education the work of the Charlotte Area's five church-related institutions of higher education was coordinated through a new council that he initiated. He did not want the colleges to become isolated unto themselves or the conference to fragment its support of the colleges. The College

Coordinating Council, complete with an executive secretary, was his effort to assure the churches' responsible support of their schools.

Evangelism, the proclamation of Jesus Christ as Lord and Savior resulting in decisions for and commitments to Christ and his reign, was an early passion of the bishop, dating back as far as Sulphur Springs camp meetings in his childhood and the evangelistic outreach from First Church, Johnson City, in his youth. He was emphatic when the statistician's report in his third quadrennium drew attention to the continuing decline in church membership. The news of decline was nothing new to church people who frequented annual conference sessions. After all, they had been hearing those reports since the late 1950s.

Hunt knew full well that the motivation for evangelism did not spring from a statistical report. Because evangelism is intrinsic to the gospel itself, the report in membership decline cast the issue of evangelism in a far more radical perspective. The report was an indication that the church was "missing the mark of the gospel somewhere, somehow." His words to the conference rang with passion:

We have done a better job with dollars than we have done with folks, and dollars are not the business of the Christian Church . . . people are. . . . I cannot believe that there are 258 pastoral charges that have received no new members on profession of faith, not even a child by way of confirmation class. . . . I have heard all of the rationales for this. I've heard all of the elaborate ways to avoid facing up to the evangelistic task. I have heard young preachers brag that they are not evangelistic. . . . But . . . any minister of a church that is unable to go out and win somebody for the Lord Jesus Christ during even a short conference year is missing the mark of the Gospel somewhere, somehow.

> . . . the first priority of this Annual Conference ought to be
> to win men and women, boys and girls, to Jesus Christ! If you
> think that's too simplistic, and if you think it doesn't take into
> consideration the sophisticated niceties of contemporary
> thought, you don't know me very well. . . . That's not where I'd
> stop but that's where I'm starting.[23]

Evangelism without a social conscience, Hunt was convinced,
was truncated, if not distorted. Early in his administration he
had led the conference in developing two new inner-city ministries in the Charlotte Area, and he had encouraged laity and
clergy in building teams of volunteers to go to other countries.
He had guided the conference through the period of the merger of the two conferences, North Carolina-Virginia and Western
North Carolina. He had seen to it that African American presence would be evident in various positions of leadership in the
conference. He forcefully called the conference to its social
accountability, but he never boasted in any self-serving way. In
fact, in later years he would regret that he had not addressed the
issues of race earlier in more prophetic ways.

In 1972 Hunt completed the prescribed limit of two quadrennia of episcopal leadership in an episcopal area. In response
to the Western North Carolina Conference's request the jurisdictional conference concurred that Hunt should serve an additional four years in the Charlotte Area. Elected at the young age
of forty-five, Hunt had a possible twenty-four years of service in
the episcopacy. Usually, exceptions to the two-quadrennium
limit are granted in the later years of tenure. The Western North
Carolina Conference had made a compelling case. The conference was in the midst of consolidating the conference offices in
Charlotte, bringing a segment of the staff from Statesville and
unifying the staff in a new headquarters in Charlotte. Julian

Lindsey states that this was an ambitious move that needed Hunt's leadership since it had encountered opposition of some magnitude.[24] Another reason for his continued leadership was the venture of the conference in establishing two retirement centers: Arbor Acres in Winston-Salem and Givens Estates in Asheville.

At the 1976 jurisdictional conference the bishop would have to move to a new area. He had completed twelve fruitful years of service in the hills of western North Carolina. He had come to the area with an evangelical mind and heart fused into one vision with the three earmarks of his North Carolina years— learning, evangelism, and social commitment. The future lay in the hands of the Jurisdictional Committee on Episcopacy with the confirming vote of the jurisdictional conference.

Nashville Area, 1976–1980

The final action of the Southeastern Jurisdictional Conference meeting at Lake Junaluska in 1976 was to receive and affirm the report of the Committee on Episcopacy regarding the placement of the bishops for the following quadrennium. Earl Hunt was assigned to the Nashville Area, an area comprising two annual conferences—Tennessee and Memphis.

The Nashville Area is a distinguished episcopal seat. In the old "southern church" Nashville was the site of the church's Sunday School Board, and even more important, it was the center of the church's publishing enterprises. With unification in 1939, Nashville had continued to be an important center of the denomination, particularly since all the publication concerns of the united church, including curriculum and the Abingdon-Cokesbury Press, were consolidated in the Tennessee city. By the 1970s Nashville was indeed one of the nerve centers of the church. Two general boards of The United Methodist Church, the General Board of Discipleship and the General Board of Higher Education and Ministry, were situated in the west end of the city. Affiliated with the Board of Discipleship was the *Upper Room,* the most widely used devotional publication in the country, as well as Discipleship Resources, serving primarily the United Methodist constituency with enrichment materials. Alongside the concentration of the church's publishing interests— The United Methodist Publishing House, Abingdon Press, and Cokesbury Book Stores—was the denomination's communications center, United Methodist Communications. Nowhere in The United Methodist Church were so many agencies of the church concentrated in one location as in Nashville. Nashville was also the home of Scarritt College, an institution of higher education sponsored by the Women's Division.

Nashville had been a seedbed of early Methodism. Bishop Francis Asbury conducted his last conference in 1816 near Lebanon, Tennessee, before dying in Virginia. Earlier the Nashville Area had been a geographically extensive area embracing three annual conferences—Tennessee, Memphis, and Holston. In 1968, however, Holston had become a separate episcopal area. Now comprised of two conferences, the Nashville Area presented real challenges.

The Tennessee Conference was well contained within state and natural boundaries. The Memphis Conference stretched from the Mississippi border in the south into southern Kentucky. Historically, the conferences had had somewhat different histories. Clustered around the hub of Nashville, the Tennessee Conference had experienced a pattern of administrative consistency. On the other hand, at times the Memphis Conference had been a part of the Jackson Area (Mississippi), and at other times a part of the Louisville Area. The geography had tended to set the boundaries of the conferences and to a considerable extent had shaped their histories. Each conference had its distinctive ethos. The Tennessee Conference with Nashville as its center had been influenced over the years with the presence of staff members of the boards and agencies taking active roles in the life of the local congregations. The Memphis Conference was noted for its homogeneous, almost family-like character.

The conferences had long histories of institutional responsibilities. The Memphis Conference took great pride in the Methodist Hospital in Memphis, as well as Lambuth College in Jackson, the Reelfoot Rural Ministry in Obion County, Tennessee, and the United Methodist Neighborhood Centers in Memphis. The Tennessee Conference claimed Martin College in Pulaski and a host of community ministries. In short, any bishop's administrative skills would be challenged in such a rich and diverse area.

The two episcopal areas, Charlotte and Nashville, were distinctly different. Hunt had ready support and guidance as he began to negotiate new episcopal waters. Edward L. Crump Jr. was superintendent of the Memphis Conference's Paris District for Hunt's first two years in the area. In 1978 Crump would be transferred to the Tennessee Conference to become pastor of the Belle Meade Church in Nashville. Crump and Hunt had a common background in the Holston Conference, where Crump's father had served as conference youth director at the time the bishop was still a youth.

Crump recalls that Bishop Hunt always sought to be fair in the question of appointment making. He remembers Hunt as having a propensity for the dramatic in decision making. "Crises" always seemed to be on the horizon.[25]

One time, however, Hunt was in a real crisis when he was

snowbound in the Paris District. The experience may be the origin of an affectionate nickname given to Hunt. Apparently, the bishop became much more "weather conscious" after his experience. Prone to be very cautious about weather conditions, he gained the nickname "Snowflake" from his pastors.

For the entire area Hunt appointed Lloyd W. Ramer as the area administrative assistant. Hailing from the Memphis Conference, Ramer was well equipped for the task. He had served as chairperson of the Memphis Conference Board of Ministry and had been a member of its Council on Ministries. In addition, within the jurisdiction he had been a member of the Board of Evangelism, the Jurisdictional Council, and the Jurisdictional Commission on Communications. In the general church he had served on the Joint Radio Commission and had been a member of the General Board of Missions. Ramer's wealth of experience on all levels of the connectional church as well as his strong standing in the Memphis Conference enabled him to be an indispensable assistant to the bishop.

Perhaps the biggest issue Hunt confronted in the Nashville Area was the proposal for a merger of the two conferences. The Southeastern Jurisdictional Conference had endorsed this idea at its 1976 session. The Reverend Jerry B. Carr, in commenting about the report of the Memphis Conference committee in 1979, said: "Inheriting us and our talk of merger," the bishop's "immediate task was to organize the merger committees, which had already been named, and to charge them with leading us in a thorough study."[26]

The Memphis Conference's committee made its report to the annual conference session in 1979 with the formal motion supporting merger. The report also had the backing of the Memphis Conference Cabinet. The major supporting arguments were that the merger would broaden the slate of appointment choices for congregations and increase the variety of ministries for clergy, the merger would allow for the possibility of developing a more extensive professional staff for the Conference Council on Ministries and would be economically feasible due to a combined budget, the merger would enlarge the support base for conference institutions, particularly for Lambuth College, and the merger would strengthen the influence of the Nashville Area within the jurisdiction.

When put to the vote, however, the motion to merge was soundly defeated, with 223 in favor and 345 opposed. The opposition vote no doubt reflected concern focused on several issues: (1) clergy pensions (the Tennessee Conference had a better pension rate, but the Memphis Conference had its program for pensions better funded); (2) the actual length west to east of the proposed new conference, a distance of nearly 350 miles from Memphis to Crossville; (3) concern about whether both Martin and Lambuth Colleges could continue to be supported adequately; and (4) concern about whether the merger would tend to cut off the Kentucky part of the conference with the possibility that the Kentucky sector would eventually be assimilated into the Louisville Conference.

One week later the Tennessee Annual Conference met in Clarksville. The Tennessee Conference committee was chaired by William W. Morris (who was elected to the episcopacy in 1992). Roy C. Clark, who within a few weeks would be elected to the episcopacy, indicated that nine of the ten committee members favored merger. When the vote was taken, and the results announced, nothing had changed. By almost the same margin as reported in the Memphis vote, Tennessee voted 240 for merger and 320 against.[27]

Bishop Hunt had attempted to maintain a nonpartisan position, but many suspected that he really favored the merging of the two conferences. In any event he reported to the 1980 juris-dictional conference that all of this "exacted a great toll of intel-lectual, emotional, and spiritual energies during three of the last four years."[28]

In spite of the time and energy consumed in the merger nego-tiations, Hunt continued to press for the same advances in the two conferences that he had stressed in Western North Carolina—education, evangelism, and social responsibility.

Addressing the Memphis Annual Conference in what would be his final session with them in 1980, he outlined what he con-sidered to be the priorities for the immediate future in the con-ference. On education, he said, "I can't image hope for the future without a rediscovery of higher education in church col-leges" and called upon the conference to recognize the respon-sibilities in "educating our youngsters today." On evangelism, he noted: "The membership of United Methodists in the Memphis Conference was 107,329 in 1979. Since 1974, the conference rolls have decreased by a total of 5,548 members." The loss of membership was equal to the membership of the three largest churches in the conference. He urged that each member go out determined to "bring one soul to Christ during the coming year." On social responsibility, the bishop called for education of the laity in Christian social concern, saying that the church must be at the center of changing and improving racial relationships. He was to the point: "We also must remember the horror of Nazi Germany during World War II and its desire for a superior race. We cannot be unconcerned about the rise of the Ku Klux Klan in recent months."[29]

One week later Bishop Hunt made his valedictory state-of-the church address to the Tennessee Conference. He chose as his medium his best form of public address—a sermon. Taking a "double text," one from Ephesians 5:14: "Therefore he said,

Awake thou that sleepest, and arise from the dead and Christ shall give thee light," and one from William Cowper:

> Where is the blessedness, I knew,
> When first I saw the Lord?
> Where is the soul-refreshing view
> Of Jesus and His word?

he embarked upon one of his most carefully crafted sermons. Shades of Western North Carolina and Memphis Conferences could clearly be detected now in the Tennessee Conference.

On education, he specifically dealt with the conference's support (or lack thereof) for Martin College: "Martin is an integral part of the Tennessee Conference life, *quite as important to the conference as the conference is to it.*" On evangelism, he gave one of the most passionate appeals of his entire ministry. He exclaimed:

> We may have allowed the deep, historic meaning of most of our big words in religion to become so tragically eroded that they are little more than what William James used to call "bloated absolutes." One of these, by our deliberate wilfulness, is "evangelism." Others—more important—are its components: "Sin," "Salvation," "Faith," etc. Our allusions to these fundamental terms of the Gospel, at best, are abstractly theological and innocently literary—rarely probingly personal. This is surely one reason why the eleven o'clock worship service, as the late Samuel Miller put it, is almost supremely "a place where the bankruptcy of modern ecclesiasticism is apparent." . . . What I am saying is blunt and elemental—and perhaps certain to arouse the ire of those who do not wish to hear it: For God's sake, get your own life and heart right with your redeemer. Go back to the springs of your faith and drink deeply of their refreshing and renewing

waters. Review the fundamentals, and preach and testify about
them. Then will something thrilling happen in your Sunday
morning church service; then will troubled, frightened, lost people faltering and stumbling in the sophisticated darkness of the
70s, see a great light and know the salvation of their Lord. I dare
to ask it again: *Do you really have a gospel to share? Getting one
is the only effective answer to the evangelistic problem.*[30]

As for social responsibility, the bishop appealed to his people,

Most of us are deeply convinced that the Christian not only has
an obligation to the starving around the world, but also a responsibility to recover the virtue of austerity in his or her own personal life. It is greatly to be hoped that we shall comprehend the
need for a fundamental revision in life-style compatible with
New Testament patterns, and that such a revision, accomplished
on corporate levels, will attack both waste and inequitable distri-
bution of food resources.[31]

Addressing the issues of race, he continued,

Racism of any form within any part of the human family is blas-
phemy against God and a denial both of Christianity and fundamental Americanism. It would be unthinkable to me that there
should still exist in this Annual Conference a single congregation
of United Methodist people where a person of another race
would not be warmly welcomed as a guest or a member.[32]

A motion by Joe Pevahouse, lay leader of the Memphis
Conference, had been presented to and passed with enthusiasm
by the conference a week earlier. It read:

A request for the re-assignment of Bishop Hunt to the Nashville
Area for another quadrennium is recorded in the recent minutes

of the Conference Council on Ministries, the Conference Committee on the Episcopacy, the Memphis Conference Cabinet, and the delegation to the Jurisdictional Conference.[33]

Pevahouse wanted to be sure that all the bases had been covered and properly recognized. One week later Dr. Robert Spain (another Tennessean to be elected to the episcopacy in 1984) made a motion directed to the Jurisdictional Committee on Episcopacy, stating "the Nashville Area's continued pleasure of the leadership of Bishop Earl G. Hunt, Jr., and desire that he be re-assigned to the Nashville Area in 1980, and as long thereafter as possible."[34] As in Memphis, so in Nashville. The motion carried overwhelmingly.

But come the jurisdictional conference in July, other considerations would overtake the motions of the two conferences, and Hunt would be assigned to the Florida Area.

Florida, 1980–1988

Some in attendance at the final session of the jurisdictional conference registered surprise when Earl Hunt was assigned to Florida. He had served the Nashville Area one quadrennium, and both conferences had registered their strong desires that he be returned for another four years. Within the jurisdiction a rumor had circulated that a newly elected bishop would be assigned to the Florida Area. Floridians seemed to be fond of newly elected bishops. The last four bishops—Short, Branscomb, Henley, and McDavid—had been assigned to the area immediately following their elections. Hunt, on the other hand, had a sixteen-year record of experience in the office.

Unquestionably, a major consideration for the Committee on Episcopacy was the fact that Hunt had eight more years to serve before retirement. Students of the episcopacy generally agree that a one-term bishop is not the best deployment of the church's resources. Whatever the consideration of the Committee on Episcopacy–in most instances never known to the jurisdictional conference delegates–Hunt was on his way to Lakeland, Florida, and a new venture in episcopal experience.

The geography of Florida sharply contrasted with that of the Charlotte and Nashville Areas. No misty peaks of the Smokies of Western North Carolina and no rolling hills and the Mississippi flowing past Memphis defined the new territory. From the red clay fields of northern Florida to the sandy beaches etched by the tides of the Atlantic on the east and the Gulf of Mexico on the west, Florida was different. Once he was settled in the Sunshine State, no longer would "Snowflake" have to fear the icy roads of winter.

More important than geography and weather, United Methodism in Florida possessed a different character from the bishop's two preceding areas. Historically, the church in Florida was younger, yet with a considerably larger number of older adults than in North Carolina and Tennessee. Not only had Florida received waves of "snow birds" and retirees from the North; in recent years thousands of refugees from the Caribbean, particularly Cuba, had swelled its population. The venerable large churches such as First Church, Orlando, and Christ Church, St. Petersburg, were now exceeded in member-ship by newer suburban churches populated largely with baby boomers and their children. Florida was different from the more traditional cultures of the mountains and valleys of North Carolina and Tennessee, with their longer-established towns and villages exhibiting the mores and social behavior steeped in history.

Even the sociopolitical climate was different. In North Carolina and Tennessee, Hunt's position on racial integration and civil rights had roused opposing voices. His advocacy of the Equal Rights Amendment had not been greeted favorably in all quarters. Furthermore, his opposition to capital punishment had for a long time sparked questions about his political positioning. They had never risen to the level of real controversy, however. Initially, Hunt misread the Florida political climate. Floridians may not have had the long history of time and place, which North Carolinians and Tennesseans claimed, but they were not any less traditional on many issues. Upon arrival in Florida, Hunt participated in some newspaper interviews in which he expressed himself on these and other issues. He received a substantial number of messages of criticism regarding the social and political views he had enunciated in the press. On the other hand, many laypeople and clergy of the Florida Conference were ready and willing to back their new bishop, even if he did need a good orientation session to the new climate.[35]

Even the episcopal residence was different from former ones. It was situated on the banks of Lake Hollingsworth and adjacent to the modernistic Frank Lloyd Wright campus of Florida Southern College, a conference college. The episcopal office had been designed as a part of the residence. When the cabinet was convened, the bishop and his superintendents gathered around the dining room table. Little from his East Tennessee youth had prepared him for this new experience. New challenges and new opportunities presented themselves at every hand.

One of the first matters to receive the new bishop's attention was not a new frontline missional issue but conference finances. For a number of years the operational budget funds and the endowment funds had been commingled. Consequently, the conference had been borrowing from its endowment to complete its operational budget. Nearly two million dollars were owed to the endowment. In cooperation with conference leaders Hunt set himself to the task of restoring fiscal solvency. Fiscal solvency was mentioned prominently in the bishop's reports to the conference. The financial dilemma was not resolved until Hunt was well into the second quadrennium. The financial condition put serious limits on the implementation of the bishop's hopes and aspirations for the conference.

The financial crunch did not dampen Hunt's spirit. At his first annual conference (May 25-29, 1981), surrounded by a galaxy of bishops including Edward J. Pendergrass Jr., James W. Henley, John Wesley Lord, Richard C. Raines, and Wilbur Smith (of the Brazilian Methodist Church), the new bishop struck his themes. One by one the items on his agenda reverberated from the walls to the ears of the people filling the Branscomb Auditorium on the Florida Southern campus.

"I want this great Annual Conference to move forward in the important area of church extension. . . . The world is literally moving into our state, and I want us to build new churches wisely, strategically and boldly. I want us to welcome as a creative opportunity," he continued, "our ministry among the refugees who have come to our shores. . . . I want us to be prepared as a Conference to articulate intelligent, courageous Christian positions on all social and human issues which throng the horizon today."

Then he turned to his persistent theme across seventeen years of episcopal tenure: "I want us to have better preaching. . . . Our people need to go to church on Sunday confident in their belief that they will receive some fresh message from God which will enable them to live through the days of the next week with greater strength, courage, and peace."

As much as, if not more than, any other conference in the jurisdiction the Florida Conference had witnessed in recent years the rise of the charismatic movement within its churches.

In some churches tensions and conflicts had arisen, while in other churches the spirited witness of charismatic Christians had renewed evangelistic zeal and invigorated worship. Hunt spoke for harmony and understanding: "I want the charismatic movement and every other good movement of our Church to work together in spiritual harmony here in the Florida Conference. . . . We must take the great power which is in the charismatic movement and turn it into those channels which will enable us to accomplish the high objectives of New Testament Christianity."

As persistent as the bishop's appeal for better preaching was his call for a deeper commitment to evangelistic witness. "I want us to evangelize," he almost shouted. "While there are factors over which neither a local church nor a national denomination has much control, there is one factor peculiar to the Christian over which she or he does have control, and that is the gospel's call to meet the neighbor, friend or stranger with a word about Jesus Christ."

Bringing his address to its climax, he assured the conference, "God Himself will join you and me in our accomplishments in terms of all these hopes and dreams. And it is a task big enough to command everything that Heaven has in the way of resources and all that we can offer in the way of human skills and dedication. God let it happen!"[36]

These were stirring words to many of the Floridians as the conference attendees rose to their feet to applaud their new bishop. Frank Furman, conference lay leader who in the Florida years was one of Hunt's right-hand deputies, led the conference in its enthusiastic response. One conference pastor, Ben Rider, moved that the "excellent and timely remarks of Bishop Earl Hunt be printed in the Florida Methodist and as a permanent record in the Journal and be distributed to the media." The motion passed, and with a road map the bishop's second year was about to begin.[37]

The 1972 General Conference had approved a report of the Legislative Committee on Membership and Evangelism calling upon the Council of Bishops to issue a statement on the work of the Holy Spirit. This was in response to the rising influence of the charismatic movement in the church. The Standing Committee on Teaching Concerns of the Council formed a task force including a representative from each jurisdiction and the overseas conferences and the current president of the council. Hunt was chosen to coordinate the efforts of the task force, the results of which were published in 1974 with the title *Storms and Starlight: Bishops' Messages on the Holy Spirit.*[38] In the preface to this collection Hunt attempted to put in context the bishops' studies and messages, juxtaposing the church's "storms" and "starlight." Under a canopy of the church's confession of faith in the triune God, many different experiences of the Holy Spirit could contribute richly to the church's life if guided by its faith in the triune fullness of God. The bishop's analysis, however, revealed that "we have gone from the extreme of ignoring the Spirit to the opposite extreme of emphasizing the Spirit almost to the exclusion of the other two Persons in the Trinity, and in so doing have threatened the church with what amounts to another form of Unitarianism."[39] The solution was not a rejection of any movement of the Spirit, but a recovery of theological sanity. The stirrings of the Spirit in recent times were to be affirmed while exercising caution as to some of usages to which the experiences had been directed. Drawing from his storehouse of memory, the bishop recalled the statement that the late Bishop Arthur J. Moore was reputed to have said on more than one occasion: "A fanatic is never a person with too much religion, but rather someone with too little sense!"[40]

That was precisely the bishop's approach and method as he sought in his own conference to mediate between charismatics and traditionalists when matters became heated. He attempted to hold the various viewpoints within the spectrum of the historic evangelical faith, seeking a *via media* by which the church could continue to live in unity and mission. The role the bishop played in these matters was easily subject to misunderstanding and criticism. Some traditionalists felt that he "gave" too much to charismatics, and at times some Spirit-filled Christians perceived him to be an ardent institutionalist.

As with a range of issues across his ministry Hunt sought to be a "bridge figure." Such a posture is indeed a vulnerable one, subject to criticisms from all sides. In Hunt's case, the criticisms frequently failed to fathom what really was working in the bishop's mind. Like his theological mentor, John Wesley, Hunt was convinced that an evangelical core allowed for a variety of appropriations and practices. What he sought to preserve was what Wesley had called "the marrow of faith." As long as the core doctrines (triune God, incarnate and atoning Christ, Holy Spirit, salvation by grace) were affirmed there could be a variety of appropriations and practices as long as these contributed to the building up of the Body of Christ. In the case of the charismatic experience, he did not seek to discredit the experience, but he did insist upon rational judgment as to the uses to which the experience was put. In such disputes and conflicts his effort was to put into practice what Wesley had called the "catholic spirit."

In 1956 the General Conference had voted for full ordination rights and conference membership for women. Hunt strongly supported his church's stance on the ordination of women. Across the years of his episcopacy his sermons and addresses give evidence of his having taken seriously the use of inclusive gender language when speaking of the human family. In Florida he periodically called the women clergy together to discuss such issues as appointments, maternity and paternity leaves, and other related matters. The method of cautious consultation had been a mark of his episcopal administration in the two preceding episcopal areas. Bishop Joe Pennel, who served under Hunt in the Memphis and Tennessee Conferences, observes that it was a style the bishop had learned well in his college presidency days.[41]

By 1987 Hunt was ready to appoint Florida's first woman district superintendent. He chose Charlene Kammerer, a person of proven administrative skills. Among her other responsibilities, Kammerer was a member of the General Board of Global Ministries, and her administrative abilities there would be recognized in the next quadrennium when she would be elected to head, within the membership of the board, the section on United Methodist Overseas Relief. Kammerer would in 1996 become the first woman to be elected to the episcopacy in the Southeastern Jurisdiction.

The church's ministry with Hispanics in the Florida Conference received high priority on Hunt's agenda. Toward the end of his eight-year tenure in Florida, at a rally of Hispanic Methodist congregations at Olympia Heights church in Miami, the achievements of the Hispanic congregations were celebrated: a 580 membership increase, $400,000 increase in offerings, five churches reaching self-support, seven laymen and laywomen serving as district officers, four delegates to General Conference, ten persons serving as conference officers, two new day-care centers, three new missions, and twelve candidates for the ordained ministry.

Evangelism continued to be one of the bishop's priorities, as it had been in the two preceding episcopal areas. By the conclusion of his two terms in Florida some modest indications of church growth could be measured. While in some areas of the country membership continued to decline, only Florida and a few other boom areas were recording increases. The Florida Conference reported adding nearly 8,700 persons to its rolls in 1987 but lost 7,700 through death, transfer, or the clearing of inactive members from church rolls. The net gain of less than 1,000 raised the conference's total membership to just under 340,000.

As Hunt surveyed the wider church, he reflected, "The great revivals of religion and the startling examples of church growth are now taking place in parts of the world that were once mission lands. The mainline Protestant denominations in the United States appear to be moving into an almost irreversible decline as they did in England and other countries earlier."[42]

His analysis of the malaise of the denominational churches pinpointed what he perceived to be the root causes. Television evangelists discredited evangelism in the eyes of many persons, posing "a severe ethical problem for thoughtful church leaders and an actual threat to many of the established churches endeavoring to do unselfish ministry." The major influence he saw to be the rising tides of secularism, resulting in the "elevation of affluence," reflected in the materialistic attitudes of both clergy and laypeople. "Many churches today seem to regard installing cushions in their pews or paving their parking lots as more important than giving money to missions."

Another problem he spotted was what he termed "privatization," defined as the practice of every individual determining for himself or herself what is of ultimate significance. "Individually, none of us can be arbiters of the content of Christianity." Turning specifically to his own United Methodist Church, the bishop believed that the denomination was suffering because it had drifted away from the theology of its founder, John Wesley.

For Wesley, Scripture was the central measure of truth, but "we have allowed ourselves to lose that. . . . We became weak in our Christology, weak in our understanding of the doctrines of sin and salvation, and we almost abandoned the Holy Spirit."[43]

The bishop nevertheless had not lost hope. "I agree that some of those who have left our church have felt that the church left them first," he said. "But I think now our church is awakening to that fact. You can see it in the new church school curriculum, in the new generation of ministers coming out of our seminaries and in a new thrust by the Council of Bishops to develop discipleship and strengthen the local church."[44]

The local church and its ministry were always in the forefront of the bishop's concerns. When he arrived in Florida, almost immediately he began to lay the foundations for an institute on preaching similar to the one he had established in Western North Carolina. He had persistently reported the desire of laypeople for better preaching. Through the generosity of Mr. and Mrs. Frank W. Sherman, a United Methodist lay couple of Jacksonville, he initiated the Florida Conference Institute on Preaching.

The Florida Conference had the ideal facilities for the institute in its conference center located in Leesburg. No other conference in the church could claim better conference and camping resources. Within the structure of the institute's program, the J. Wallace Hamilton Lectureship on preaching was given a central role. Hamilton had started the Pasadena Church in the 1950s, and it had become famous as the "drive-in" church. Naming the lectureship for Hamilton was one way for the conference to memorialize one of its esteemed members. So well were the foundations of the institute laid that it has continued to be an important date on the calendar of Florida pastors in the years after Hunt retired.

Hunt's characteristic advocacy of church-related higher education was unabated in Florida. Within the bounds of the conference two such institutions were located: Florida Southern College in Lakeland and Bethune-Cookman College in Daytona Beach. Each institution had a distinctive mission. Florida Southern had over the years been the conference's college in terms of relationship and support. Bethune-Cookman was nationally recognized as an outstanding African American college and was supported by various conferences of the church, including Florida. Dr. Robert A. Davis, president of Florida Southern, found a strong ally in Bishop Hunt, even urging him to remain in Florida after his retirement and assume consultant responsibilities with the college. This invitation Hunt regretfully declined, citing his strong conviction that pastors and bishops should refrain from continued presence in former assignments.

For the eight years of his Florida tenure Hunt served as the chair of the board of Bethune-Cookman College. This historic college had been founded and guided by the vision and personal labors of the distinguished African American educator Dr. Mary McLeod Bethune. When the bishop retired in 1988, he culled through his personal library, separating out the volumes that would be appropriate for an undergraduate liberal arts college. He gave this collection to the library of Bethune-Cookman, a school whose historic mission he so strongly endorsed.

The connectional church beyond the boundaries of his episcopal areas called the bishop to additional responsibilities, at times extraordinarily heavy ones, and the years of his Florida tenure were no exception. He served as president of the General Board of Higher Education and Ministry from 1980 to 1984. He was a member of the Governing Board of the National Council of the Churches of Christ from 1972 to 1984 and of the Executive Committee of the World Methodist Council from

1976 to 1986. In addition he served as chairperson of the American Section of the World Methodist Council from 1982 to 1986. In 1984 the General Conference voted to establish a new Committee on Our Theological Task, and Hunt was selected to guide this committee through the quadrennium as it forged a new theological statement in preparation for the 1988 General Conference. The latter responsibility was particularly demanding. To compound matters, Hunt was elected president of the Council of Bishops for the year 1987–1988. These responsibilities required him to be absent from the conference periodically (for days at times).

Upon his arrival in Florida, Hunt had found his seminary classmate Durward McDonell in the position of administrative assistant to the bishop. McDonell had been appointed by Bishop Joel McDavid, and Hunt was delighted to have him continue. During his later years in Florida, Hunt chose Roland Vanzant for the position. Both McDonell and Vanzant rendered Hunt and the conference valuable service.

His last quadrennium in Florida proved to be the busiest of his entire twenty-four-year tenure. Vanzant, who had been a district superintendent, relieved Hunt of many administrative tasks and freed him to meet the wider church's demands. One member of the cabinet at this time relates that it was a significant learning experience for many in the Florida Conference. Many came to a better understanding and appreciation of the wider church and its mission through the bishop's engagement in these activities.

The Florida years were drawing to a close. At the 1988 jurisdictional conference Hunt would make his final report on this episcopal area and would retire from the active episcopacy. The Florida Conference prepared well for the 1988 sessions of the annual conference. The Floridians were proud of their bishop and intended to express their appreciation with particular acts at the time of the conference. Two events in particular stand out. One was serious, the other more lighthearted and jovial. Early in the week the bishop delivered his final state-of-the-church address to which the conference responded with a standing ovation. Following the Wednesday evening session honoring the retiring pastors and at which Bishop Robert M. Blackburn, a native Floridian and resident bishop of the Richmond Area, preached, Frank Furman and his Retirement Committee led the conference in a reflective, yet amusing, program. A slide presentation outlined the life and ministry of Bishop Hunt, and a delightful video interview with Mrs. Hunt, entitled *A Bishop's Wife Speaks Her Mind,* was shown. The district superintendents were called to the stage and performed a dance called "The Earl" done to the music of "The Duke of Earl." Mrs. Eva Pollock Love, a classmate of the Hunts from 1935 to 1937 at Science Hill High School in Johnson City, Tennessee, shared some entertaining vignettes of their youthful days.

The Hunts were escorted to the stage and presented with a package containing more than 1,600 autographs from delegates and friends of the annual conference. Hunt happily received the collection of autographs to begin a new collection, since he had already sold his earlier collection. Furman concluded, "You don't say good-bye to people you love. We simply share our heartfelt thanks and appreciation." The conference rose to its feet singing "God Be with You 'Til We Meet Again." The Florida years were rapidly coming to an end.[45]

Dr. James Laney, president of Emory University, and Dr. James Waites, dean of Candler School of Theology, had invited Bishop Hunt to be Bishop in Residence and Visiting Professor of Evangelical Christianity at Candler, and he had accepted. Bishop Hunt's supportive Florida layman, Frank Sherman, had volunteered to fund this position at Candler for as long as the university and Hunt desired. The Hunts anticipated their move to Atlanta, but Hunt experienced an illness that would prevent his assuming these new academic responsibilities. In September 1988 the Hunts moved to their retirement home at Lake Junaluska, that "Mecca of Southern Methodism!"

Mr. and Mrs. Earl G. Hunt, Sr., at the old family farm, Sulphur Springs, Tennessee, in November 1941.

The Hunts were married on June 15, 1943, and reported to Earl's student charge for duty three days later. This was taken outside Sardis Methodist Church in Atlanta on their first Sunday there.

Earl, Jr., with his father in 1945. In the background is the seventy-five-year-old farmhouse to which the Hunts were appointed in Chattanooga, Tennessee. This young church, Wesley Memorial, had 37 members at that time.

Dr. Robert E. Speer, famous Presbyterian missionary statesman, addressed the Johnson City Youth Council in 1940. Left to right, Rev. Robert Parsons, Becky Stevens, Earl Hunt, Dr. Speer, Dr. Robert C. Rankin.

President Hunt and chaplain Dr. William C. Mason flank the famous missionary Dr. E. Stanley Jones at Emory & Henry College in 1961.

President Hunt and Chaplain Mason with Dorothy Maynor, famed American musical artist, who appeared in the Emory & Henry Lyceum program in 1963.

Four presidents of Emory & Henry. From left to right: Dr. William C. Finch, Dr. Charles Sydnor, Dr. Thomas F. Chilcote, Jr., and Dr. Earl G. Hunt, Jr.

Newly chosen bishop-elect Dr. Hunt is escorted to the Stuart Auditorium platform by Bishop Roy H. Short and Bishop Arthur J. Moore in July 1964.

Acting President and Academic Dean Dr. Daniel G. Leidig with newly elected Bishop Hunt at Emory & Henry College, August 1964.

Bishop Hunt and Bishop Edgar A. Love of the former Central Jurisdiction reading jointly the Proclamation of Unification that brought together the Western North Carolina Conference and a large portion of the NC-VA Conference in 1968. In the background are two prominent lay women of the United Conference, Mrs. Jettie Morrison and Mrs. Murphy Nelson.

Dr. James Calvin Peters, Sr., the first African American District Superintendent in the Southeastern Jurisdiction. From left to right: Dr. J. W. Gwyn, Sr., of Saint Paul's Church in Winston-Salem, N.C.; Bishop Hunt; Dr Peters; and the Honorable Richard Erwin, Federal Judge, now retired.

Hunt with part of his beloved autograph collection. (Photo from Hunt's private collection. Photo by Charlotte News, Elmer Horton, 7/12/73)

Bishop Hunt was installed as Resident Bishop of the Nashville Area (Tennessee and Memphis conferences) in autumn 1976. Bishop Roy H. Short spoke, and leaders in both conferences were on the platform.

Archbishop Fulton J. Sheen, famed Roman Catholic prelate and TV personality, was one of an array of distinguished speakers for the Western North Carolina Homiletical Institute. Here he is greeting the Hunts.

Bishop Michael J. Begley of the Charlotte Diocese of the Roman Catholic Church and Bishop Hunt were warm friends during Hunt's Charlotte residency, helping their churches to work together in different ways including prison ministry.

Bishop Hunt with former President Gerald Ford and Dr. Robert A. Davis, President of Florida Southern College at a campus event.

Bishop Hunt with former President Jimmy Carter and
Dean James Waites of Candler School of Theology.

Archbishop Desmond
Tutu and the late Dr.
Spurgeon Dunnam with
Bishop Hunt in Nairobi,
Kenya, in 1986.

Bishop and Mrs. Dale
White and Bishop and
Mrs. James K.
Mathews with the Hunts
in Nairobi, Kenya, 1986.

The retiring President of the Council of Bishops, Bishop James Mace Ault, handing the Episcopal gavel to Bishop Hunt in April 1987.

Bishop Hunt, Dr. Ralph W. Mohney, first Distinguished Evangelist in Residence at the General Board of Discipleship, and Bishop Edward L. Tullis, Chair of the Foundation for Evangelism Advisory Board.

The Hunts celebrated their golden wedding anniversary with a dinner at Grove Park Inn on June 15, 1993, with close friends of the years. From left to right: Dr. and Mrs. Ralph W. Mohney, Bishop and Mrs. Robert F. Lundy, Dr. and Mrs. Ben St. Clair, and Mrs. Wava Teilmann, widow of Dr. Gunnar J. Teilmann, Jr., Earl's seminary roommate.

The Florida Bishop and Mary Ann at the end of the line!

Three presidents of The Foundation for Evangelism: Dr. Charles Kinder, Bishop Ernest A. Fitzgerald, and Bishop Earl G. Hunt, Jr.

Steve, Edeltraut, Mary Ann, and Earl Hunt, Lake Junaluska, N.C., July 1997.

Chapter Five

❦

Bridge Builder

*D*uring the years 1972–1976, The United Methodist Church undertook a study of the episcopacy through the means of an Episcopacy Study Commission set in place by the General Conference. After extensive interviews with all of the bishops, the commission issued its report. Among other findings the commission's study revealed that episcopal leadership style is multifaceted. The church at large knew this, but the commission's work brought clarity to the matter of varying styles of leadership. Like a carved stone or gem, a bishop's leadership style has a number of sides, each worthy of consideration. But generally, one characteristic stands out from the others, exhibiting a dominating and unifying trait. The various characteristics are gathered around this one dominant characteristic. Hence, some bishops are known as institutional administrators. Others are recognized as pastors to pastors. Some bishops are known primarily for their preaching abilities, giving voice and direction to the church from the pulpit. Some are noted for scholarship and intellectual depth. And still others are seen as social prophets.

Preacher, educator, and apostle of evangelism are distinct traits of Earl Hunt's leadership, but the one integrating center has been his bridge-building efforts in the various spheres of his episcopal activity. He has sought to be a reconciler or mediator in a church of diverse claims and convictions. Across his ministry he has sought to bridge the gaps between evangelicals and liberals, evangelism and education, piety and social responsibility. While efforts have been made to force his image into one or the other—evangelical or liberal, evangelist or educator, pietist or social transformer—he has stubbornly resisted the "or" and persisted with the "and." Above all else, he has sought to be a bridge figure in the church.

A bridge is a complex, yet fundamentally simple, structure. A paradoxical combination of tensile strength with tremendous carrying power makes a bridge an essential transit between two points. Grand and complex as its structure may be, the function of a bridge is quite modest and simple one of facilitating the flow of traffic from one side to the other. Paradoxical and complex, simple and modest, these are the necessary characteristics of the bridge-builder model of episcopal leadership.

The church needs episcopal leaders who are catalysts and change agents. A static church is a dying church. But the church also needs episcopal leaders who help the church navigate the churning waters of differing convictions and perspectives. A vital church dwells in unity in the midst of its diversity. The character of the episcopal leadership of Earl Hunt has unmistakably been that of reconciler, mediator, builder of bridges.

The *Book of Discipline* defines the office of bishop as one of superintendency. From 1784 to the present the shape of the general superintendency of the church has evolved and changed. The office of general superintendency or bishop was a powerfully specific one in the earliest days of American Methodism. At the close of the eighteenth century and the advent of the nineteenth century, there was no ambiguity regarding the office and its powers. Francis Asbury defended and utilized such powers with determination. The powers of the office included the right of appointment, not subject to review, of the itinerant preachers; the rights to ordain deacons and elders (including veto power in the matter of ordination) and to consecrate other bishops; and the right to prevent a preacher from publishing or circulating literature antagonistic to the church. The bishop was educator of clergy and editor of the publications of the church; presider over sessions of conference; and supreme law officer who could act as an appellate court on matters of denominational law. The range of power was considerable, and the definition of the office quite specific.

The church in 1830 suffered division, in part due to the issue of episcopacy, though the primary protest of the Methodist Protestants had to do with the rights of lay representation in conference. Slowly but surely, the office of bishop was refined, and the scope of powers was reduced principally to matters of appointment. By 1939 the Methodist Protestants could join the Methodist Episcopal and Methodist Episcopal South churches in a union of the three branches. So changed was the office that Bishop Straughn could testify "that he marched from Methodist Protestant presidency to Methodist episcopacy without missing a step."[1] At the same time new duties emerged. Bishops were to endorse and lead new programs, crusades, and missional emphases, accompanied at times with General Conference attempts to limit episcopal tenure and even on one occasion to strike the term bishop from the *Discipline* and substitute general superintendent. Is it any wonder that Bishop Embree Hoss could opine in 1918, "I have many duties but no prerogatives"?[2]

Murray H. Leiffer identified several changes in the authority of bishops in The Methodist Church between 1940 and 1960. Among them were (1) quadrennial emphases, which took from the bishop responsibility for program making, and (2) the requirement of consultation with the cabinet in appointment making.[3] Commenting on the same period, Frederick Norwood notes the primary reason for the changes: "A force of increasing influence was the collective power of the administrative secretaries of the national boards and commissions. The bishops became aware—unhappily—that much of the leadership in developing quadrennial programs rested in the hands of the Council of Secretaries and the Coordinating Council."[4] This picture of the changing and limiting of the role of bishops is further complicated by the divided mind of the general church. The 1972–1976 Quadrennial Commission for the Study of the Offices of Bishops and District Superintendents reported that one of the paradoxical revelations of its research was "the suspicion of leadership joined with the cry for leadership."[5]

In the midst of these "shifting," "confusing," and "paradoxical" developments, Bishop Short commented to the Council of Bishops, "The only real power that any United Methodist bishop has is that which flows out of the example of his/her life and character as well as demonstrated qualities of church leadership."[6] The modern bishop will be remembered less for his or her bold, new strategies, administrative decisions, and eloquent sermons and more for the projected image of character that the bishop brings to the office.

Spanning twenty-four years of episcopal tenure, Earl Hunt witnessed not only these institutional changes but also the emergence of new stresses and tensions involving such issues as the increased role of ethnic and special interest caucuses, human sexuality (particularly homosexuality), ecumenical relations (attacks upon the National Council and World Council of Churches and increasingly the shift from conciliar to grassroots ecumenism), growth and vitality of the church in the Two-thirds World and the decline in membership and public influence of the American church, and theological pluralism (hailed by some and equally disdained by others). Hunt's official duties brought him to the center of these tensions and potential polarities within the body of the church.

Human character is forged and shaped in the matrix of many different powers of influence. Such was certainly the case with Hunt. The years of his childhood and youth were permeated with a form of southern Methodist evangelicalism that was at once Christocentric without being doctrinaire, ecumenical without compromising loyalty to his own church and tradition, revivalistic while at the same time socially sensitive, particularly to situations of economic injustice, and theologically conservative while incorporating the best of the liberal tradition. His seminary years at Candler introduced him to new approaches to biblical interpretation. He enrolled in every course that Franklin Parker taught in systematic theology. Parker, whose theological approach was more of an apologist than a critic, grounded him in the great doctrines of the faith. At the same time, Hunt was attracted to W. Aiken Smart's New Testament lectures. Smart, a Union Theological Seminary graduate, was perceived by some in the church to be "too liberal" theologically and socially to be elected to the episcopacy. Hunt's character was formed in the environment of forces that tugged and pulled at each other but in the final outcome managed to keep the poles in creative, interactive tension without courting contradiction or reductionism.

Within the Council of Bishops, Hunt claimed Bishop William Cannon as one of his closest friends. No one questioned the theologically and socially conservative credentials of Cannon. At the same time, Hunt had an almost hero veneration for Bishop G. Bromley Oxnam, "the paladin of liberal Christianity," and Hunt spearheaded almost single-handedly the Council of Bishops' project of Oxnam's biography.[7]

Within the wider church, Hunt served on the Governing Board of the National Council of Churches from 1972 to 1984, a body frequently charged by some to be "liberal." In 1971 he was a featured speaker at the Good News movement's convocation. He could count many friends in the Good News movement, "a forum for scriptural Christianity" within The United Methodist Church, though he was never officially a member of the organization. In 1983 he appeared on a forum with Richard John Neuhaus and Paul Ramsey; the sponsor was the Ethics and Public Policy Center in Washington, a conservative think tank whose president was Ernest W. Lefever. During the same period, he continued a warm relationship with President Jimmy Carter. In 1994 he delivered the principal address in Dallas commemorating the life and ministry of Dr. Edmund W. Robb Jr., a United Methodist conference evangelist and conservative activist. Among his many activities, Robb was the founder of the Institute for Religion and Democracy (IRD). The IRD has been a watchdog of the boards of The United Methodist Church, especially the General Board of Church and Society and the General Board of Global Ministries, and a critic of the National Council of Churches, a forum that Hunt championed.

Some observers chalk up the bishop's activities as evidence of vacillation. Others accuse him of pragmatic expediency. Either criticism fails to understand the various forces that had shaped the bishop's character over the years. What on the surface may appear to be inconsistencies reveal in essence a mind that thinks conjunctively rather than disjunctively, a disposition inclined more toward the "and" than the "or." Hunt's style of leadership had little affinity with antithesis (either/or) or synthesis (both/and). His whole background prepared him more for the dialectic (push/pull). The push/pull equipped him with the tensile strength of a bridge, which allows for traffic in both directions and the possibility that the interaction of the traffic will ultimately produce a stronger unity. He loved bridges more than chasms. The record can be documented with his episcopal activities in the wider connectional church, though at times, there are significant exceptions.

A consideration of the one major exception makes clearer Hunt's general drive to forge bridges. Between 1967 and 1972 Bishop Hunt was the chair of the General Committee on Family Life. The Section on Marriage and Family Ministries of the Board of Discipleship was conducting workshops on human sexuality in various quarters of the church. Suddenly, the activity of the workshops broke in the public press. Among the many resources used in the workshops were "sexually explicit" films. A clamor was heard from various voices in the church. Hunt reacted quickly to denounce the use of such resources, and the films and the workshops ceased to be.

During the same period, the Committee on Family Life recruited a task force to write a new document on family life for the church. Members of the task force came from various sectors of the church. When the first draft of the report was completed, the draft found its way into the hands of the secular press. A leading weekly news magazine ran an account citing the report's definition of marriage as a covenant relationship "between two persons." The reporter chose to interpret this as a covert espousal of homosexual relationships. The bishop again moved quickly to summon two members of the writing team, James Wall of *Christian Century* and James Logan of Wesley Theological Seminary, to St. Louis where the matter was clarified, and the final report would read "a covenant relationship between a man and a woman."

Hunt was attempting to steer the committee through the thicket of a host of controversial issues confronting the church.

The world outside the doors of the committee's deliberations was seething, and at times erupting, with what the popular press called "the sexual revolution." In his leadership of the Committee on Family Life Hunt sought to make secure the church's traditional stance on family and sexuality. He did not ignore the cultural changes and contemporary lifestyles. But the church's theological and moral position, he strongly held, was rooted in other soil than that of contemporary terrain, regardless of how much at variance with social practice the church's position may be.

In the restructuring of The United Methodist Church in 1972, Hunt's General Family Life Committee ceased to exist. Memories differ about exactly what happened. Tensions between the Family Life Committee and some staff members in the Section on Marriage and Family Ministries of the General Board of Discipleship had continued since the conflict over the films. Did the tensions have anything to do with the demise of the Family Life Committee? Others remember that the Committee on Structure, in preparing its report for the 1972 General Conference, considered that a Committee on Family Life outside the Board of Discipleship and a Standing Committee on Family Ministries within the board constituted a redundancy. Memories aside, the Family Life Committee that Hunt had led for five years no longer existed. Hunt recalls that the committee was unpopular "because of its alleged conservatism." The General Conference's restructuring meant that the committee died a silent death, and "there was no opportunity for a final meeting," Hunt remembers. The Committee on Family Life had been engaged in initial explorations about suitable study material on a Christian perspective on homosexuality. These explorations continued after the Family Life Committee no longer existed, and in 1981 the General Board of Discipleship published a small study book, *Homosexuality: In Search of Christian Understanding*,[8] stating that the work was the result of action by the Family Life Committee and the Standing Committee on Family Ministries of the Board of Discipleship.

In the meanwhile homosexuality and related issues surfaced in the 1972 sessions of the General Conference. In the same year *Motive*, a journal for college students of the former Methodist Church, devoted its last two issues to a discussion of homosexuality. The ferment in the larger society was evident within the church itself. The 1972 General Conference positioned the church by declaring that "homosexual persons no less than heterosexual persons are individuals of sacred worth." They are entitled to the ministry and guidance of the church and are to have "their human and civil rights ensured . . . though we do not condone the practice of homosexuality and consider this practice incompatible with Christian teaching."[9] That had been essentially Hunt's position as he led the Committee on Family Life.

Hunt's views on family life and human sexuality have remained consistently traditional. On the issue of homosexuality, he has maintained his support of the church's position first stated in 1972 and reaffirmed in subsequent General Conferences. Ironically, what was viewed by many as a moderate position in 1972 is now looked upon by some in the church, including some in the Council of Bishops, as a conservative one.

During the year 1987–1988 Hunt served as president of the Council of Bishops. Midway in his one-year term he addressed the council as the church prepared for the 1988 General Conference.[10] He enumerated the key issues that he saw before the church. He could have muted his concerns, but his address was specific rather than general, hard rather than conciliatory. He struck forcefully at the issue that he had addressed all the way across his tenure—racism. Here he received no resistance in the council. He was preaching to the choir. On the issue of homosexuality, dynamics were different. At the close of his address many bishops arose and applauded his remarks; others remained seated. The council was obviously not of one mind.

When Hunt's address to the Council of Bishops was reported in the press, his comments on homosexuality were widely discussed in the church. He notes having received more than five thousand letters. The volume of mail was so great that temporarily he had to hire an additional secretary to handle the correspondence.

Differences in the council became public in 1996 when fifteen members of the council issued a statement to the press on the eve of the General Conference sessions in Denver expressing their discomfort with the church's current position on homosexuality. They considered the position too conservative. Hunt was disturbed with their position and equally disturbed that such an unannounced public statement outside the confidentiality of the council violated the council's integrity and compromised the age-old position of the church that at General Conferences bishops are "to be seen and not heard," particularly when it comes to influencing legislative issues before the conference.

On issues of family life and sexuality, Hunt has maintained his traditional stance. His positions on these issues mark the rare exception to his general disposition to be the mediator and healer of breaches. His position was firmly set on these issues, and he could not find the moorings requisite for the building of bridges.

In 1972 Bishop Hunt became a member of the Governing Board of the National Council of Churches, a position he held for twelve years. Founded originally as the Federal Council of Churches in 1908 to bring the Protestant churches of America into united service for Christ and the world, to secure a larger combined influence for the churches in matters affecting the moral and social conditions of the times, and to promote the application of "the law of Christ in every relation of human life," the council was reorganized in 1950 to include the Orthodox churches, as well as the Armenian church and the Polish National Catholic Church. From the beginning the intentions of the council had been ecumenical cooperation, particularly related to the vexing social developments confronting the church and the nation. Its purpose was functional rather than organic union of the churches. The character of its actions and pronouncements had always been of a social nature. Its first general secretary was the Methodist pastor Frank Mason North, famous for penning the words "Where Cross the Crowded Ways of Life." In fact North's hymn could well have served as a poetic statement of the council's purpose.

The National Council was the object of vocal criticism and attack. The volume swelled to its highest decibel point in the 1950s when the council was accused of being infiltrated by Communists. One United Methodist annual conference, South Carolina, conducted an investigation and, after a painstaking sifting of all available facts, concluded, "After considering all of the matters called to the attention of the committee, we are unable to substantiate a charge of communism, communist domination or communist sympathy within the ranks of the National Council of Churches."[11]

In the 1960s the council positioned itself in actively support-ing the civil rights movement in the South and opposing the country's military engagements in Vietnam. From outside the council critical voices were raised to protest the council's posi-tions on these issues. Many of these voices represented forces which had never favored such an ecumenical venture as the council in the first place. In addition, voices from individuals and groups whose churches held membership in the council rose to oppose its positions on these same issues of race and war. Many of these complaints came from the South, Hunt's native soil.

Hunt's appointment to the council was a strategic one for the church. No one questioned his theological soundness, and he came from an area of the church least favorably inclined toward the council. When he spoke, his voice could be heard with credibility. And speak he did.

The United Methodist house organ, *Interpreter,* carried an article by Hunt in 1975 in which he defended the council and countered its critics:

> Some of these belligerent critics undoubtedly have been well-intentioned (although misinformed). It is still a fact, however, that some critics upon occasion have used their battles against the National Council to augment their own treasuries through the generous financial response of good local church members who have been persuaded mistakenly that they were thus engaged in a sacred warfare.[12]

The council printed thousands of copies of Hunt's statement and distributed them throughout the various member churches.

After citing the council's efforts in disaster relief primarily through Church World Service, its agricultural and medical missions, its international evangelism forums, its refugee resettlement program, and its ministry to migratory farm workers and to vacationers in our national parks, Hunt concluded that if the church did not have a National Council of Churches, it would have to create one of necessity. He reminded United Methodists that the oldest continuous broadcast in the world had been the National Radio Pulpit, which featured the late Dr. Ralph W.

Sockman, a lifelong Methodist. The council cooperatively supported the interchurch efforts for the weekly broadcast known as The Protestant Hour, where numerous Methodist preachers, including Hunt, were given nationwide exposure.

Hunt concluded, "Let us begin to think more positively of the National Council of Churches, and support with our prayers, our study and our constructive criticism this important and distinguished arm of the Christian enterprise in our day. Perhaps there is no better immediate way to implement our Lord's own aspirations as revealed in his great high-priestly prayer."[13]

Repeatedly in print and public forum, he stood in the breach defending the council, United Methodist participation in it, and his personal endorsement of it. Many United Methodists in the local church were of more conservative social persuasion, and he attempted to bridge the gap through a fair interpretation of its program coupled with his credible character.

Back in his own episcopal areas, Hunt pursued the same course of building bridges in the midst of rising criticism of the institutional church for stands that the larger church championed:

A great many of our folk are so confused and disturbed over a cluster of current happenings that they are allowing their faith in the Church itself to be shaken. . . . A few, without realizing or acknowledging the fact, may be taking out on the Church and its leaders the anger and resentment they actually feel toward the political structure of the country and those who guide it in these tempestuous times. They may sense that they can get at the Church easier than they can the nation.[14]

He confessed impatience and anger at times over some things said and written, allegedly in the name of the church:

But I do not become impatient and angry enough to jeopardize the future of the Church in a world which needs its witness so desperately. By such criticisms manifested in the withholding of financial contributions the ground can be cut from under those leaders who are struggling to correct the very errors which disturb so many. The danger is that a loyal opposition can unwittingly fall into at least one of three possible groups: the radicals who are striving to bring revolutionary destruction to all worthwhile institutions in society, including the Church; irresponsible reactionaries who stand to gain by promoting their own agendas; and those who unknowingly adopt measures similar to those measures employed by the ideologies which they oppose. Finally, one can imperil one's own life by surrendering to the bitter and debilitating spiritual poison of a negativism which is aware of all the problems but unwilling to search constructively for any of the solutions.

The bishop's prayer for his people was, "God help us to bring the Church safely through its crisis!"[15]

Hunt's ecumenical engagement was not confined to the national scene and the American church. From 1976 to 1986 he was a member of the Executive Committee of the World Methodist Council. This body is a forum for the various churches of the world Methodist family, including the three African American Methodist churches as well as the Wesleyan and Free Methodist churches in the United States, the British Methodist Conference, and the various autonomous Methodist churches in Africa, Asia, and Latin America.

Hunt was invited to be the keynoter for the thirteenth assembly of the World Methodist Council, meeting in Dublin, Ireland, in August 1976.[16] The program chairman, Bishop Dwight Loder, had emphatically instructed him that his address could be no longer than twenty-nine minutes. On the platform he stood between Dr. John Havea of Tonga, a member of the presidium and physically a giant of a man, and the dignified representative of the Lord Mayor of Dublin (who, Hunt recalls, left before he had begun his address!).

The address before the World Methodist Council struck the characteristic themes of Hunt's messages at home. In Dublin, though, he knew his audience well enough to sense that they were more consciously Wesleyan than his American Methodists. He vigorously espoused three Wesleyan emphases. First, there was assurance of sins forgiven: "One thing wrong with the Church today is that it has too many good and respectable people in its pews and pulpits who have never known the unmitigated horror of sin's conviction or the inexpressible wonder of forgiveness and deliverance. The song of Aldersgate is strangely absent from our repertoire."[17]

The second emphasis was on the realization of sanctification in the here and now. The unworthy habits of the heart must be rooted out, and that can happen only by the power of Christian regeneration. Salvation involves the cultivation of impulses, desires, and feelings of Christian character, what Wesley called the growth of the "holy tempers." Sanctification, for Wesley, was no arid doctrine but a lively process embracing the whole of character, firing it into a passion for love and justice in the world. Hunt reminded the British in his audience that William Booth had once commented that real religion is "like a cup of tea—no good unless it's hot."[18]

The third emphasis on social redemption followed naturally. Hunger, racism, the Bomb, the disintegration of family life, drugs and drink, poverty, the lack of affordable housing, the tortured struggles of people seeking freedom, identity, and dignity, the incredible excesses of affluence—"these are problems that no child of God dare attempt to escape."[19]

For ten years Hunt devoted what time he could squeeze from his busy schedule to take an active role in the World Methodist Council. He was convinced that American Methodists in particular, and Americans in general, had a propensity to become parochial. Only consistent contact with a world church could prevent that malady. During this period, he did not address himself to issues in Pan-Methodism, such as conversations between the African American Methodist bodies in the United States and The United Methodist Church or dialogues with the holiness churches that sprang from the Methodist stem in the nineteenth and early twentieth centuries. These developments had not yet occurred. The World Methodist Council, Hunt was convinced, was the one forum through which these diverse bodies could maintain contact with each other. Upon the completion of his tenure on the Executive Committee of the World Methodist Council, he was awarded the World Methodist Chair of Honor in recognition of his leadership.

Whether it was the National Council of Churches or the World Methodist Council, Hunt saw these as inter- and intra-forums for ecumenical advancement. Whether "inter-" or "intra-" they were means for bridge building.

Hunt claims that "the most important assignment" of his ministerial career came during the last quadrennium of his active work. The 1984 General Conference may be known in the history books as the "General Conference of the Commissions." Coming as it did on the two hundredth anniversary of the church's founding, the conference established two quadrennial commissions—one on the perennial issue of the ordering of ministry and the other on the mission of The United Methodist Church. In addition, in response to a request from the legislative Committee on Discipleship, the conference called for the Council of Bishops to form a Committee on Our Theological

Task, with the instructions that the committee "prepare a new statement that will reflect the needs of the church, define the scope of our Wesleyan tradition in the context of our contemporary world, and report to the 1988 General Conference."[20]

The church had addressed this issue previously in the quadrennium of 1968–1972. The so-called Outler committee (the late Albert Outler chaired the committee) presented its report to the 1972 conference. The committee had not addressed the issue of a new formulation of doctrine for fear that such effort would be in conflict with Restrictive Rules 1 and 2 of the Constitution. Rather, the committee presented a carefully phrased statement on theological method. United Methodists could claim that their theological distinctiveness lay in the manner in which they thought theologically more than in actual theological or doctrinal content. The result was the famous Quadrilateral statement on Scripture, tradition, experience, and reason. Although Wesley himself had never combined the four explicitly, on occasion he wrote of "Scripture, tradition, and reason." This formulation was characteristic of the Anglican *via media* going back to Richard Hooker and other Anglican divines. The methodological statement was in keeping with the spirit of the times. In 1968 the former Evangelical United Brethren and the Methodist churches merged after an intense methodological quest for union. The church was "method conscious."

Another feature of the 1972 report was its endorsement of "theological pluralism" as descriptive of The United Methodist Church. As early as 1974, Dr. Schubert Ogden of Perkins School of Theology argued that the report, passed by the General Conference with little debate and no amendments, was obscure or ambiguous because it displayed a "certain confusion" as to the nature and task of theology. The report had argued that theology was a matter of "free inquiry" within the parameters of the

Quadrilateral or methodological guidelines. On the other hand, the report spoke of theology as "doctrinal reflection and construction" within the framework of a Wesleyan heritage. Especially with Ogden's first observation, if theology is a matter of "free inquiry" within the four guidelines, theological pluralism is the logical outcome.[21]

Between 1972 and 1984, voices not limited to the reflective centers of the theological schools raised concerns. Without a more specific delineation of the church's theological heritage, the church faced a severe problem in identity. Even though Outler had intentionally used the phrase "theological pluralism" in order to make a place within the church's spectrum for conservative theological voices, the loudest cries for a new theological statement came from the church's conservative voices. The uneasiness with the 1972 statement was manifesting itself over a wider constituency of the church. Ogden, a leading process theologian, was no conservative. In general many in the church sensed that in a time of cultural and societal uncertainty, the church needed a more specific statement.

The membership of the 1984 Committee on Our Theological Task, appointed by the Council of Bishops, included five bishops, five academicians, five clergy, five laity, and four at-large members. Its membership was balanced in terms of race, gender, age, and geography (representatives from European and Pacific areas). Hunt had been asked by the Council of Bishops to convene the committee, and at the first meeting on February 18-19, 1985, in Atlanta, Hunt was elected its chair. Other officers included Dr. Richard Heitzenrater, Perkins School of Theology, vice chair, and Mrs. Mai Gray, former president of the United Methodist Women, secretary.

The committee met five times over the quadrennium for extended intensive sessions. Heitzenrater, a highly regarded historian of the Wesleyan movement, emerged as the chief drafter of the report. Two other seminary professors, Dr. Thomas Ogletree of Drew and Dr. Theodore Runyon of Candler, were resourceful in providing the technical historical and theological background that the committee needed. The committee's membership was broadly representative of the United Methodist theological spectrum. The sheer theological variety of the committee's membership called for Hunt's bridge-building skills and consumed much of his time and energy. Otherwise, the committee could have disintegrated, providing a disappointing parable for the entire church.

Hunt guided the committee, under the guidelines of the General Conference, seeking continuity with the earlier report while gaining consensus with the General Conference's expectations. The General Conference action had specifically listed three issues to be addressed: (1) the significance and proper use of the so-called Methodist Quadrilateral; (2) the proper understanding of the catholic spirit, which is often spoken of as pluralism; and (3) the contribution that United Methodism can make to the ecumenical-theological conversation. Specific criticisms of the 1972 statement would have to be addressed. Within the committee were persons who articulated those criticisms as well as those who argued vigorously to "stick with" the 1972 statement.

For some the notion of the Quadrilateral was unclear. Literally speaking, a "quad" could be made to rest on any one of its four sides. Was this the intention of the 1972 statement? The principle of theological pluralism could lead to apathy or indifferentism in the church. Some on the committee insisted to the contrary. For them the theological pluralism of the church was a liberating and creative experience. The fact that the 1972 statement seemed to downplay "doctrinal standards" to "landmark documents" was troubling to some. What are the "doctrinal standards"? In fact, what is the nature of doctrine itself? To what extent are standards "juridical"? The earlier statement had actually said that doctrinal standards were "nonjuridical." A primary task of the chair of the committee was to interpret such questions and help the committee to clarify them. Some questions had to do with historical practice and precedent. Other questions were more theologically explicit. Still other questions, such as the juridical nature of standards, had to do with polity. Hunt was responsible to keep these levels of discourse—historical, theological, and procedural—untangled and clarified, while seeing to it that every concurring and dissenting voice in the committee had a fair hearing.

Hunt advised the committee to go "public" with a preliminary draft of its report in the February 1987 issue of *Circuit Rider.*[22] He knew the church. While the array of conflicting responses might be disconcerting to the committee, a public reading of the committee's work was necessary if the report were to have credibility in the church.

Critical responses were almost immediate. The group gathered around the Houston Declaration of 1986 were gratified to see their language of "the primacy of Scripture" appear in the report. On the other hand, Dr. John B. Cobb Jr., of the Claremont School of Theology faculty and a member of the 1972 commission, exclaimed in the May 1987 issue of *Circuit Rider,* "I say, 'Keep the quadrilateral!'" Cobb saw a fundamental change from the 1972 statement: "Basically it is a shift from presenting the four members of the Wesleyan quadrilateral (Scripture, tradition, experience, and reason), as each independently important and as richly interconnected, to sharply separating Scripture from the other three, emphasizing its sole primacy and subordinating the others to it."[23]

Dr. Kenneth C. Kinghorn of Asbury Theological Seminary, a member of the Good News movement, and a member of the committee, argued, "The church needs authoritative guidance if it is to rediscover its way. We can trust in our own wisdom, or else we can turn to a divine source beyond ourselves. . . . Part of Wesley's success lay in his unshakable confidence in Scripture as a non-negotiable source of authority."[24] The Reverend David E. Conner, pastor of the Estes Park church in Colorado, perceiving that "the pluralistic quality of our theology is now being attacked," argued that "what is crucial to see is that a theological style which emphasizes each individual's own experience of God requires a degree of flexibility and 'latitude' in order to accommodate the inevitable element of personal perspective, which individual experience entails."[25] At least the committee's preliminary report helped to clarify where the lines in the church were drawn. Hunt had already anticipated these very lines. After all they were present in the committee itself.

To complicate matters further, a scholarly controversy erupted involving the committee's vice chair, Dr. Heitzenrater, and Dr. Thomas C. Oden of the Theological School of Drew University. In the fall of 1985 Heitzenrater had published a long scholarly article in *Quarterly Review* claiming that when the Constitution of the church, in particular Restrictive Rule 1, was adopted in 1808, the early Methodists intended that only the *Articles of Religion,* not Wesley's *Standard Sermons* and *Explanatory Notes Upon the New Testament,* be covered with constitutional protection.[26] In fact, the Heitzenrater thesis was incorporated in the committee's preliminary draft. Oden, a theologian and Wesleyan scholar of conservative proclivities, entered the fray in the spring 1987 issue of *Quarterly Review.*[27]

Oden, a prolific writer, followed with a book, *Doctrinal Standards in the Wesleyan Tradition,* published in the early spring of 1988, hoping that it would have an impact on the General Conference. Oden mustered an array of constitutional commentators, some more reliable than others, to support his case that the Wesley *Sermons* and *Notes* had always been considered doctrinal standards in American Methodism. As chair of the committee Hunt faced an open disagreement between his own vice chair and a person with considerable influence in conservative quarters of the church. If the report were to be a "consensus document," many more hours of deliberation and drafting were needed.

Hunt convened the final meeting of the Committee on Our Theological Task in Oklahoma City in October 1987. Heitzenrater's drafting committee had met in July, and several drafts had been written and rewritten in preparation for the full committee's meeting. The committee fine-tuned the document and sent it to the secretary of the General Conference. A major achievement had been accomplished. The committee itself had come to a consensus and fully supported the report. Hunt's diplomatic efforts combined with the efforts of other members of the committee had paid off.

In April 1988 the General Conference delegates descended upon St. Louis. Already it was known that a new legislative committee would be constituted specifically to deal with the reports from the Committee on Our Theological Task and the Commission on the Mission of the Church. Already there were the predictions of doom that such a diverse church could never reach a consensus on matters as essential as doctrine. In some instances theological positions had hardened into political factions.

Hunt knew the political lay of the land and worked the halls contacting key persons from the various factions of the church. He attempted to clarify the work of his committee and to dispel the rumors circulating in the hallways. He deployed Heitzenrater and Ogletree to the legislative committee. To the best of their abilities, they were to interpret the document to the legislative committee. They then kept Hunt informed about the progress of the discussions and debates.

The newly constituted legislative committee on Faith and Mission, which received the doctrine report, was chaired by Dr. Thomas Langford of Duke University. Throughout the first week Langford led the legislative committee through a painstaking examination of the doctrine report, paragraph by paragraph. The largest observer galleries of any legislative committee were to be found hanging on the words of debate in the Faith and Mission sessions. The final result was overwhelming approval by the legislative committee. A consensus had been achieved!

The consensus depended on the resolution of the tensions that had developed in the church's response to the report. Before the General Conference convened, Heitzenrater and Oden in one sentence had resolved the matter of the doctrinal documents by recognizing that the 1968 *Plan of Union* had included the *Articles, Sermons,* and *Notes.* The issue on "the primacy of Scripture" was handled by breaking down the Quadrilateral into separate divisions beginning with a section entitled "Scripture." The legislative committee authored its own opening paragraph: "United Methodists share with other Christians the conviction that Scripture is the primary source and criterion for Christian doctrine. Through Scripture the living Christ meets us in the experience of redeeming grace. We are convinced that Jesus Christ is the living Word of God in our midst whom we trust in life and death."[28]

Probably the most significant development, though not thoroughly understood by many of the delegates, was the distinction made between doctrine and theology. That was already implicit in the report submitted but was made explicit by the legislative committee. The statement read: "Our doctrinal affirmations assist us in the discernment of Christian truth in ever-changing contexts. Our theological task includes the testing, renewal, elaboration, and application of our doctrinal perspective in carrying out our calling 'to spread scriptural holiness over the lands.'"[29]

Langford attempted to explain this distinction between doctrine, on the one hand, and theology, on the other, with an analogy based on the architectural structure of a house and modification and renovations of the house. Doctrine was comparable to the structure, while theology was the church's task within the house. This distinction permitted a normative role for the church's doctrinal tradition while allowing for a diversity of theological approaches within the same house.

Cynics claimed that the dropping of "pluralism" and the adoption of "diversity" were mere "word play." Dr. Dale Dunlap, former dean of Saint Paul School of Theology, in the conference's plenary session hailed this distinction as the genius of the report, for it allowed the church to hold to a doctrinal distinctiveness while not freezing its theological reflection into theological rigidity.[30] The report passed the General Conference with a favorable vote of more than 97 percent. At least for the moment the church could celebrate that some political and theological divisions had been bridged. Hunt took pride in his committee's accomplishment while always insisting the committee's achievements would have been impossible without the persistence of the vice chair, Richard Heitzenrater.

A year before his retirement from active episcopacy the bishop reflected over the nearly twenty-four years of his tenure. The result was a book published in 1987 entitled *A Bishop Speaks His Mind: A Candid View of United Methodism*,[31] which sought to cover the waterfront of the denomination's opportunities and shortcomings. Hunt considered the issues grave, and occasional-ly, his oft-used word *crisis* appears.

The book was not greeted with accolades in some quarters of the church. His intentions had been conciliatory, but at times Hunt's rhetoric was "hot." The book was punctuated with state-ments such as, "I approach this discussion with a full awareness that the problem is difficult, delicate, and complex, but with the hope that concerned church leaders like myself may find a way to bring a desperately needed reconciliation between these viewpoints."[32] Reconciliation had been the driving force in much of Hunt's ministry. How would his readers respond?

His critics tended to see only one side of his dialectic. Bureaucracy was defensive when he voiced his suspicions that the General Board of Global Ministries (GBGM) "seemed to have adopted as a primary objective infiltrating and changing political and social orders, with a secondary emphasis on win-ning people to Christ."[33] He attempted "to right" the balance by drawing attention to GBGM's "almost unbelievably varied min-istries." Then he appealed for dialogue leading to reconciliation between the board and the Mission Society for United Methodists. Hunt had twice been an interlocutor in efforts to bring the two bodies together. He worried about the lobbying presence of the bureaucracy in the General Conference, even suggesting that the boards and commissions might consider a reduction in the number of staff members present at General Conference. He pondered the possibility that the church was near a "paralysis of structure."

Hunt waded into the theological and ideological controversy over "liberation theology." His basic fear seems to have been that some forms of liberation theology advocate replacing the capitalistic system with a socialist one. He nevertheless insisted that capitalism in the United States urgently needed radical reform. While criticizing the infiltration of the boards, commissions, and theological schools with liberation theology, he did not distinguish which liberation theology. An accurate description would admit that there are liberation theologies—black, feminist, Hispanic, Asian, and African. Their distinctive differences need careful analysis and delineation. His militant language about some liberation theological endorsements of violence and the overthrow of the present economic system seemed overdrawn to some. He recognized that at times his language was "hyped."

His liberal side desperately wanted to keep before the church its social responsibility for the welfare of the hungry, the desperately poor, the unemployed, the homeless, those unable to provide necessary medical care for their families or themselves, and the aged and the frightened. Unmistakably, his call was for a Christianized capitalism. Some of his critics saw only "capitalism" without its qualification.[34]

On the other hand, he welcomed the rise of a "new evangelicalism," which was intellectually acute and socially engaged. Within the ranks of Methodism the new evangelicalism puts new focus upon the Wesleyan theological tradition. "I believe," he wrote, "it is the kind of evangelicalism that reflects Wesley's own incredibly rich repertoire of Christian convictions that our church so desperately needs today. This would correct those unfortunate aberrations that some evangelical expressions have espoused in recent years and would bring the mind and heart of our church back to what Bishop Arthur J. Moore liked to call 'the central certainties.'"

The bishop attacked the process of episcopal elections. He had earlier voiced concerns regarding the elections. Now in his book he expressed his fears quite straightforwardly: "Its principle is more political than Christian, and there are within it the latent dangers of mediocrity and, much worse, tragic error."[35]

The concern about episcopal election processes is sometimes coupled by his critics with his essentially conservative position on caucuses and quota systems. Nowhere can there be found the place where Hunt links these two. He gloried in the racial, ethnic, and gender diversity in the Council of Bishops. However, he may not have fully appreciated the process through which these persons came to the council. While there may well be some self-serving bickerings and political maneuvers by caucus groups, they have tried to hold the church accountable to its professions of inclusiveness.

Within Hunt's "candid view of United Methodism" he included some of the emphases that had characterized his tenure as a bishop. Christian higher education, evangelism, better preaching, and social responsibility are to be found in his critical survey. These were not the lightning rods that attracted the criticism of the book. In virtually every case he cited, he endeavored to balance the ledger from both sides.[36] Upon reading the book, President John Silber of Boston University commended a bishop for speaking candidly about his church. Silber, however, concluded, "Hunt is more an Erasmus than a Luther!"[37] The response to the book certainly indicated that he had touched on some tender points in the body of the church.

Many times the perceived image of Hunt is that of a conservative institutionalist. Superficially, such an image is possible. To some, his massive physical frame topped with his snow-white hair projects the proverbial image of the "southern colonel" *sans* mustache and goatee. His eloquent Victorian rhetoric can at times remind one of a time gone by. His stance on sexual ethics is unapologetically traditional. On other issues, such as racism, sexism, ageism, nuclear armament, and the economic rights of the poor, he presents a prophetic image in the best of his Wesleyan tradition.

One of his more liberal colleagues in the council depicts him as one who shares a passion for the gospel "that has made him a mighty preacher of the Word. He also shares his gift for hearing and understanding various points of view, a gift that has made him a minister of reconciliation throughout the connection."[38] Bishop Hunt is not first a theologian or a prophet (though he is both). The bishop with his "crises," real or imagined, is first and foremost a builder of bridges over troubled waters.

Chapter Six

Preacher

BEFORE THE WORD
For Bishop Earl Hunt

By Daniel G. Leidig

When he rises up in the pulpit,
the white head bowed, the mouth set firm
there is a barely perceptible shitfing:
the East Tennessee feet plant themselves,
the big shoulders lean into leather,
and all is made ready to turn the earth.

He has yet to look up.
The text is shuddering through a giant presence
like Leviathan shouldering the sea.
Then the eyes lift; we follow them,
ready for Advent, Epiphany.
Surely the Kingdom of God is at hand.

---

*P*reaching is the one, single key that unlocks the door to the complexity of issues characterizing the bridge-building ministry of Earl Hunt. The proclaiming of the Word stands at the center of his passionate concerns about the church. For him, preaching is not one activity among others on the multifaceted agenda of the ministry of the church.

Preaching is preeminent because this act summons the church into being. The preaching of Peter, Paul, and others at Pentecost marks the birthday of the church. At Pentecost it is the message, "This Jesus whom you crucified, God has made Lord and Christ," that evokes repentance and leads to baptism. The kerygma or proclamation calls the church into being as a community of the faithful. The heralding of the gospel is both the origin of the church and the reason for the existence of the church. Without the proclamation of the Word there is no church. Equally without proclamation there is no compelling mission of the church.

The plea of the laity, "Please send us a better preacher," was heard at almost every hand as the bishop consulted with his people. Their constant request weighed heavily on the bishop's conscience. As much as the laity, he wanted good preaching. The cry of the laity had even greater gravity when coupled with Hunt's view of the church, which claimed the announcement of the good news as the one essential identifying mark of the church. Preaching was vital to his understanding of the church's mission, whatever shape mission would take in any given situation. Preaching could not be divorced from evangelism, education, or social reform. Without preaching, the church's identity was threatened, causing the church to look like one more sociological institution alongside an array of other institutions of good intentions.

Given these convictions, it is understandable why the bishop was so concerned when in the 1960s he took note that many pastors were relativizing preaching and subordinating it to other functions of ministry. Clergy at times were tempted to subordinate the preaching office, sometimes relegating it to the lower priorities of pastoral ministry. While the clergy may have questioned preaching *per se,* the laity had no doubts about the primacy of preaching. They only questioned superficial, theologically unreflective preaching.

The 1960s evidenced strong attacks upon traditional institutions and traditional roles. Under the pressure of the times many pastors were seeking their identity as ordained ministers through other functions and less traditional definitions of their office. A study of the pastoral literature of the period is revealing. Pastoral ministry did indeed face an identity crisis. Competing images of the ministry flooded the pages of the new book catalogs of the publishing houses. Seeking a functional identity as pastor, many turned from identities historically found internally within the community of faith to seek their identity vis-à-vis the professions of the external society.[1] Hence, pastors were encouraged to find their identity in psychology and thereby image their ministry as counselor. Or others read Harvey Cox's *The Secular City* and sought identity as social activist.[2] Group process was the vogue in some circles, and with the aid of some developments in a theology of the laity, some sought to become enablers. The ferment in the ministry continued through the years, and in more recent times with the development of new management philosophies, some pastors have sought to become ecclesiastical CEOs.

Hunt read the times, and his interpretation was that preaching had been decentered in the minds of many pastors, though not of laity. The chaotic times had caused a failure of nerve in preaching due for the most part to a loss of confidence in the preaching act itself. The confusion of the times and the concomitant confusion in the church were the occasion for his alarm. But these conditions were not the cause of his alarm. The cause lay precisely in his ecclesiology, his understanding of the church. If proclamation is the essential mark of the church, then the contemporary loss of confidence in preaching adversely affected every aspect of the church's life. Without solid preaching, evangelism could easily become mere membership recruitment. Without a clarion call of the gospel, mission could become humanitarian service without witness to Christ. Without the announcement of the news of the victory of Christ, ritual and worship could become mood exercises in warm, fuzzy feelings. Without a faithful telling of the story of Jesus, the church could lose sight of its reason for being. Preaching kept the memory of the church fresh and alive. For Hunt, the matter was no less crucial.

One does not have to look far to find the formative influences on Hunt's resolute conviction about preaching. He was born and reared in an environment in which the preached word was the sustenance of life. His was an oral or narrative culture. The people literally lived in family narratives combined with local cultural stories. In particular, they lived in the scriptural narrative. One did not have to offer explanatory introductions to the scriptural narratives. Even the casual churchgoer knew the narratives almost from birth.

In East Tennessee the various churches had favorite name designations for their leaders. The Baptists and Church of Christ people called their leaders "pastors." The Presbyterians had their "teaching elders." Historically, the Methodists had shied from such formal terms, choosing instead to fondly name their leaders "preachers." In fact, Sunday morning and evening worship hours were most frequently called "preaching services." Preaching missions and revivals periodically marked the congregation's calendar across the year. Church people celebrated the cycle of the church year not with liturgical seasons such as Advent, Christmas, Epiphany, Lent, Easter, and Pentecost. The church year was measured from annual revival to annual revival. Preaching simply "normed" the church.

His own Wesleyan tradition, which never formulated precisely what could be called a "Wesleyan doctrine of the church," nevertheless embodied a picture of the church that was made up of four components. Preaching was primary, and it was joined with the class meeting (nurture), the Lord's Supper (sacrament), and mission (service in the world). Drawing from this tradition, Hunt emphasized the Wesleyan component of preaching ("offering Christ") intricately related to that of mission ("spreading scriptural holiness over the land").

Culture and church tradition made powerful impressions on his consciousness. Yet there were influences peculiar to him. In the days of his youth he began what became a lifelong hobby of autograph collecting (letters, documents, manuscripts, etc.). "I acquired, often at no expense except postage," he writes, "a very large collection, including papers of presidents, kings and queens, authors, scientists, military leaders, humanitarians, clergy and many others."[3] Fifty years later when he brought closure to this pursuit, he could claim a complete set of presidents of the United States and an assortment of more than sixteen hundred other important examples.

His autograph collecting increasingly enthralled him with a sense of history, which led him to a love of biography above all the other forms of literature (though his love of British mysteries gave some competition). He acknowledged that this exposure to the lives of distinguished people was one of "the formative factors in the development of my own thought and system of values." Among Hunt's gallery of "distinguished people" was an amazing collection of great preachers and their sermons. He could count an extensive catalog of the Lyman Beecher Lectures on Preaching at Yale. The Beecher Lectures became a favorite pursuit. Becoming immersed in the lectures, he regarded the lecturers as his intimate imaginary companions. He could call the roster: Henry Ward Beecher, Phillips Brooks, Peter Taylor Forsyth, Harry Emerson Fosdick, George A. Buttrick, Ernest Fremont Tittle, Ralph W. Sockman, G. Bromley Oxnam,

James S. Stewart, Halford E. Luccock, and Daniel Thambyrajah Niles. The roster included also contemporary preachers such as Fred B. Craddock, John Claypool, and Frederick Buechner. Hunt invited Buttrick and Sockman to his pulpit in Morristown and to the chapel at Emory and Henry College. He brought James S. Stewart from Edinburgh to the Western North Carolina Conference for his Institute for Homiletical Studies.

In the summer of 1985 Bishop Hunt taught a seminar in preaching at Wesley Theological Seminary. An Episcopalian rector, then doctoral student, still recalls Hunt's entry into the seminar room without notes, and for two hours he led the students in the seminar through the theological and homiletical labyrinths of the nineteenth and twentieth centuries as reflected in the Beecher Lectures. He educated his mind and stimulated his heart with the best of pulpiteers. His fondest hope for the homiletical institutes that he established in his episcopal areas was that other preachers would catch his vision and commitment to the recovery of the power of the proclaimed Word.

The Candler years of formal theological studies grounded Hunt both theologically and practically for his future ministry of preaching. He began his studies at Candler in 1941, the year in which Reinhold Niebuhr delivered the Gifford Lectures at Edinburgh on *The Nature and Destiny of Man*.[4] On the American scene a theological transition was in the beginning stages. The period of Protestant liberal theology was waning, and what was soon to be labeled neoorthodoxy was on a gradual ascent in the major theological schools.

Theologically, the twenty-seven-year-old Candler at which Hunt arrived in 1941 had been a blending of southern evangelicalism with a tinge of evangelical liberalism, the latter particularly in its Departments of Old and New Testament. Hunt's Candler years cannot, therefore, be tracked with distinct identifiable theological lines. His biblical studies provided him with solid grounding in the content of Scripture and critical methods of interpretation. Under Parker, his theological studies could hardly be identified with theological positions, fundamentalist, liberal, or neoorthodox. Parker saw to it that his students were simply steeped in the "historic doctrines of the faith." The Candler faculty were devoted churchmen (no women were yet on the faculty) with a sincere commitment that personal faith should possess intellectual and academic integrity. The greatest contribution these years made to Hunt's formation was the understanding, to which he steadfastly adhered, that a seminary education had no terminal point but was a period of preparation of the future pastor for a lifetime of ongoing study and growth.

In the years that followed, Hunt read widely in theological literature with a mind directed more toward application in the practice of preaching than toward specifically concentrated depth. What was Hunt reading? Whom was he reading? What impact would his library building and reading program have on his preaching?

If one were to draft a summary of the theological figures who appear frequently in Hunt's sermons, a profile emerges. From the Church of Scotland, figures such as Arthur John Gossip of Glasgow and James S. Stewart of Edinburgh stand out, to be complemented by James Cleland and Hugh Anderson, both of Duke but by way of Scotland. All four represent the mainstream of Scottish scholarship and churchmanship. All four, while academic types, were leading preachers in Scotland and the United States. The prophetic European voices who would spark an American neoorthodoxy, Karl Barth and Emil Brunner and later Helmut Thielicke, complemented Hunt's library-reading regimen primarily through their published sermons. Again, these were preaching theologians. Hunt read some in the Niebuhr brothers, Reinhold and H. Richard, being particularly impressed with Reinhold's recovery of the Pauline and Reformation doctrines of sin and grace. Reinhold Niebuhr's sermons seemed to have impressed him most.

Later in life, Hunt confessed that he wished he had spent more time in scholarly biblical study. With two demanding pastorates, a college presidency, and episcopacy it is impressive that he was able to keep abreast of scholarship as he did. The profile of his reading as reflected in his sermons clearly indicates that his preference was for a theology that preached. Not for a minute did he allow his focus upon the centrality of the preached Word to be distracted.

A final area of influence—and not a minor one either—was his pastoral ministry with persons in varying conditions of life. During the period of his pastoral ministry, he recalls making a minimum of two thousand pastoral calls per year! These were in addition to calls made upon him in his study office. He had an ear for his people's stories; he was present with them in their moments, high and low. On more than one occasion he cited the words of George Ade, the famous humorist, who at one time said, "The music teacher came twice each week to bridge the awful gap between Dorothy and Chopin!"[5] He clearly understood this to be the task of the preacher: "to bridge the awful gap" between humankind and God. And no small task that is.

These formative forces converged in a fourfold view of preaching in Hunt's 1987 reflections in *A Bishop Speaks His Mind*.[6] This view affords insight into both Hunt's practice of preaching and his advice to those who would preach.

1. The Content of Preaching. The message always controls the act of preaching. Hunt does not begin with an analysis of the hearers of the Word or with a system of technique for communication. The preacher's first responsibility is fidelity to the mes-

sage that God has entrusted to the preacher. The message is embodied in the scriptural witness. Christian preaching, therefore, is always biblical preaching.

Hunt was no exegetical scholar. Nor did he practice a classical form of expository preaching where a body of scripture is expounded verse by verse and phrase by phrase. By biblical preaching, he meant preaching the doctrinal content of the scriptural text. Again, Hunt's preaching, for the most part, was not classical doctrinal preaching in which one's intention was focused upon a doctrine of the faith whereby the congregation was instructed in a systematic way as to its meaning.

Hunt begins with a text, not with a doctrine, and then inquires about the faith content of the text. What follows is doctrine derived from the text rather than doctrine supported by an array of scriptural proof texts. The preacher's question is: What word is God saying in this text? Hunt's conviction is that "the people will remember Scripture if they forget everything else (or if there is nothing else worth remembering)."[7]

Christian preaching is its own *genre*. It is not lecturing. It is not philosophical speculation. It is heralding or proclaiming the story of God's saving action for people caught in the "awful gap." Christian preaching deals with the great doctrinal themes of creation, sin, covenant, Incarnation, Atonement, Resurrection, Pentecost, and final consummation. But preaching wrestles with these themes as the great good news of God's action, which can only be announced or heralded. A preacher preaching is like a messenger running through the streets shouting as he goes rather than a lecturer engrossed in the dialectics of the academy. Preaching is the announcing of the news of deliverance from the varieties of humanly inflicted enslavement, not an exercise for people waiting to be scintillated.

That such a scriptural, creedal, doctrinal message can be simply presented is illustrated by the great preachers whose books filled Hunt's study shelves. What is more important is that his preaching exemplified this principle of scriptural and doctrinal simplicity. His many sermons were demonstrations of doctrinal integrity with communicative simplicity. For example, in 1971 he preached a sermon called "Christ's Mighty Victory."[8]

The sermon is based on the familiar christological hymn found in the Pauline text of Philippians 2:5-11. The text is a poetic summary of God's threefold action in Jesus Christ. Christ Jesus who had "the very nature of God . . . but gave it all up . . . and appeared in human likeness" (Incarnation). "He walked the path of obedience to death . . . death on the cross" (Atonement). "For this reason God raised Him to the highest place above" (Resurrection). Hunt then proceeds to elucidate the three doctrinal themes.

Incarnation. History's supreme fact is that the holy, omnipotent God cared enough to put on "for a while the garments of flesh in order that He might understand us and we might know Him." Hunt's discerning eye catches the church's difficulty from early days to the present in holding simultaneously the two poles of the Incarnation, the deity and the humanity of Jesus. "If some of the early Christians came dangerously close to forgetting His humanity, then some of us, in nearer days, have come dangerously close to ignoring his Deity. Too often have we of a more liberal tradition surrendered the doctrine of the Incarnation to those extremists of the Faith who subscribe only to fundamentalism and bibliolatry."[9]

Christ's victory in the Incarnation overcomes the limitations of our finite reason to comprehend or the sinful propensities of our hearts to fabricate idolatries. The modern age's affinity for the novel and the bizarre, resulting in lives of internal irresponsibility and spiritual stupidity, is countered with this central affirmation of the faith, the presence of the incarnate God, Jesus Christ reminding us again and afresh:

> God has betrothed Himself forever to humanity! He is not only not absent from His creation; He is forever identified with it. When the Everlasting God planned a nearer visit to earth, He chose the utterly human trails of a mother's deep anguish and a Baby's low, helpless cry for the divine pilgrimage. He might have come as a heavenly visitant in trappings of cosmic splendor with spirit-legions and a chariot made of the winds, but this was not His way. He chose the cattle-shelter, "swaddling-clothes," and the loneliness of a man and a woman. And into this situation He came in the person of His Son, Jesus.[10]

Such is Christ's victory in the Incarnation.

Atonement. The Cross has been subjected to doctrinal definitions, well intentioned but limited by human thought forms, proclaimed Hunt. Anselm, Abelard, and Grotius combined cannot fathom the mystery of the Crucifixion as revealed in the scriptural narratives. Although the mystery of the Cross is beyond theological formulae, it profoundly registers in human experience. It was love to the uttermost! The forgiveness of our sin, the defeat of our human pretentiousness, the death that triumphs over death—all these are human attempts to describe how all human frailties and rebellious sins are answered on Calvary. This is not a dialectic of human philosophy but the story of Christ and him crucified: forgiveness of sin, redemption for lost and lonely humankind. Human beings do not and cannot win this victory. Faith tells us this victory we can only receive:

> Nothing in my hands I bring,
> Simply to thy Cross I cling.

Such is the Christ's victory of Atonement.

Resurrection. Hunt was convinced that the person and work of Christ constituted the Christian's authority, redemption, and ultimate hope. If Christ's Incarnation is our authority and Christ's death is our redemption, then the Resurrection is our hope and the promise of our triumph. In the Resurrection God puts the divine seal of confirmation upon the divine actions of Incarnation and Atonement. In Albert Payson Terhune's words, "God always finishes His sentences!"[11]

The human condition of dashed hopes and illusory dreams is reflective of the fact that for centuries the acids of uncertainty, skepticism, and unbelief have made us the victims, not the authors, of despair. The Resurrection is no epilogue to the story of Jesus; it is no codicil to God's last will and testament. "It is Christ's mighty victory brought to tremendous and triumphant climax."

Preaching can defy its character and attempt to be an exciting encounter with intriguing ideas, even ideas about the Bible; it can pretend to be a lofty philosophical monologue in which the mysterious presence of the incarnate God is lost; it can be a musty treatise on morals; it can degenerate to a collection of platitudes gleaned from a recent issue of *Reader's Digest.* But that is not truly a sermon. In a true sermon there must be a burning bush, an angels' choir, a cry from Calvary, and a shout of Easter joy. Otherwise, the sermon has no power to be the means whereby human lives are changed by the embracing arms of Christ's compassion. In the place of proclamation, if one attempts to substitute treatises and lectures isolated from the narrative line of the biblical text, one instantly discovers that such literary exercises are powerless to announce the hope of a new life in Christ. Only the story of Christ's great victory—Incarnation, Atonement, and Resurrection—can do that.

The content of every sermon should be biblical and doctrinal.

At the same time, the content of every sermon should be an evangelical announcement of God's salvation. Every sermon should seek to allow the moment wherein faith is born anew in different ways in the lives of different people. Every sermon should seek to make faith possible for the hearer.

Such a sense of urgency is missing from much contemporary preaching, thinks Hunt. And he is convinced he knows the reason why such urgency is rarely to be heard or sensed. As early as his Nashville years, Hunt begins to focus on two theological issues that he sees affecting the content of preaching: the sense of urgency of the preacher and the vitality of faith of the congregation.[12] The increasingly secularized climate of the society has caused a loss of emphasis on the supernatural character of faith and the eternal dimension of the gospel. "I refer," Hunt comments, "to the possibility that many of us, ordained and unordained, have been unable to retain enough of the gospel in our own secularized minds and spirits to have anything significant to share with others in a world of lost human beings."[13] He sees this secularized climate as the major factor in a theological reductionism as evidenced in preaching.

The 1960s witnessed the advent of "death of God," "secular," and "religionless Christianity" theologies. Their advocates claimed that the older theistic views of life and history could not survive contemporary interpretations and cultural revolutions. A new and radically different road had to be taken. For Hunt, this was not first an intellectual matter; these developments were rooted fundamentally in a moral decision. Human beings had come to assume that modern people can get along very well indeed without God. Hunt considered this the "illusion of illusions."

He was, therefore, critical of Tillich's notion of God as the ground of being—as over against the idea of a deity "out there" or "up there." He likewise had nothing favorable to say about Anglican Bishop John A. T. Robinson's sensational little volume *Honest to God.* While criticizing these theologians, he also turned toward those in "the trenches" of the church. "There seem to be so many of us in the household of faith who profess belief in God but who persist in living as though he does not exist or is, indeed, absent from his creation."[14]

Whether preachers consciously ascribe to such theology, Hunt observes a loss on the part of preachers of a supernatural grounding of the faith. This is particularly noticeable in the loss of a compelling sense of authority in preaching. Preaching tends to become ethics or social commentary. Hunt confesses, "I was taught to accept theism, a doctrine of God which essentially conceives of him as a Being, a Person, both transcendent and immanent."[15]

If he detected the softening of the supernatural grounding in preaching, he also was persuaded "that one of the real problems confronting the contemporary church is its virtual loss of the ETERNAL DIMENSION OF THE GOSPEL."[16] By "eternal dimension," Hunt means fundamental convictions about the purposive meaning of history as the arena in which God is seeking to bring the kingdom of God to fulfillment, and the personal meaning of life expressed in belief in eternal life or life beyond death. Hunt is careful to note that belief in eternal life is not an "escape hatch" from contemporary social responsibility; dramatically to the contrary, in the light of eternity "everything becomes different." "Right and wrong leap into new relevance. Social crises, the sins of society, injustice, oppression, racism, greed, everything else assume new and dreadful importance."[17]

Repeatedly in sermons and addresses, Hunt has continued to hammer away at these themes. What he sees to be virtual loss in the theological content of preaching undermines the authority of the pulpit and removes the essential rationale for Christian moral and social responsibility. But more than this, the loss of the supernatural and the eternal dimension threatens to remove the essential mystery of the faith. It is secularized mentality, which seeks to rationalize the mystery, consequently reducing everything to commonplace. "Religion has ceased to be religion in many of our pulpits," Hunt declares. "We've lost our understanding of the supernatural and, in some ways, our concept of eternity. When you reduce religion to something you can understand fully and see clearly, it ceases to have what religion has to have—a sense of mystery."[18]

2. The Craft of Preaching. The crafting of the sermon requires hours of disciplined labor. Hunt never offers a statement of his homiletical method. As a student of the Beecher Lectures, he knows the importance of a clear sense of direction in the sermon, and this will come only from a conscious understanding of sermonic method. He knows the older homiletical methods of expository and doctrinal approaches, and he reads with some appreciation the newer methods of narrative and dialogical preaching. His inclinations are evident in his sermon "Christ's Mighty Victory." He inclines toward an older method. While the new methods interest him, they do not deter him. He regrets "that a contemporary reinterpretation of classical preaching designs (still amazingly effective in many situations) is not more vigorously pursued by some of the able new authors in this field."[19]

He was well acquainted with life-situational preaching, the classic illustrations of which are Harry Emerson Fosdick's sermons from Riverside Church. For Fosdick "preaching is wrestling with individuals over questions of life and death, and until that idea of it commands a preacher's mind and method, eloquence will avail him little and theology not at all."[20] Hunt is as concerned, as was Fosdick, that the content of the sermon engages the real-life dilemmas with which the congregation struggles.

The difference between the two, Fosdick and Hunt, is nevertheless real. For Fosdick the method was essentially "homiletical counseling." In contrast the method for Hunt is "homiletical announcement." For Hunt preaching does not begin with an analysis of the human situation to which must be matched a theological answer. Rather, preaching must begin with the biblical text and proceed to announce the saving action of the God of redeeming love seen in Jesus Christ. In preaching the biblical text interprets the human condition; it is not the human condition which interprets the text. Hunt's strong conviction was that the depths of human life and experience are revealed and illuminated by the test as in no other way. After all, sin is a theological word, and only God and God's action can properly define and diagnose the fatal condition.

Hunt was unquestionably familiar with so-called popular topical preaching, where a current topic is taken as the subject and the biblical and theological resources are deployed in elucidating the selected topic. Hunt never commented upon this approach to preaching, which indicates that he had little sympathy with it.

Every preacher needs to know and practice a method, or else the preacher's sermons will lack structure, issuing in confusion. A clearly developed outline is necessary. If homiletical method is a matter of providing a broad road map for the sermon, enabling the hearers to have a clear sense of the direction of the sermon, an outline traces out the more minute details of the major contours. In other words, the homiletical method projects the major course of the sermon, and the outline assists in bringing the discipline of ordered thinking to bear on the structure of the sermon, preventing side roads from becoming major thoroughfares or, worse, dead ends.

Hunt insisted in teaching sessions with his pastors that every sermon should have a prepared manuscript. He did not necessarily advocate preaching from a manuscript, though he was well aware that many prominent preachers did preach from one. The use or disuse of a manuscript in preaching was a matter of style. He was concerned with the crafting of the sermon. Without the development of a manuscript, the sermon would be wanting in logical development and the intricacies of lively, captivating rhetoric. The lack of imaginative rhetoric, he observed, is one of the most telling deficiencies in contemporary preaching.

Once the sermon is "on paper," the preacher may make direct or indirect use of it in the act of preaching, or the preacher may preach entirely without the aid of the manuscript. One matter is certain. Hunt is no advocate of extemporaneous preaching. At times such preaching may be necessary, but these are the exceptions to the rule. Much extemporaneous preaching is a thin, yet revealing, cover for lack of preparation. He likes to recall the admonition of Bishop Edwin Holt Hughes in addressing a class of young candidates for ordination. "The most dangerous thing that can ever happen to you," Bishop Hughes warned, "is for you to discover that you are able to speak extemporaneously!"[21]

3. The Person of the Preacher. Phillips Brooks, in his Lyman Beecher Lectures, gave his famous definition of preaching as the presentation of truth through personality.[22] Preaching always has a medium, and the indispensable medium is the person of the preacher. To raise the question of the "person of the preacher" is, in fact, to raise the issues of integrity of character of the medium, the preacher.

Hunt observes that in recent years pietism and moralism have become "bad words" in theological circles. To some extent, he recognizes, this is understandable, given the fact that many honest people have been "turned off" by the "violent misuse of the preaching event" in the forms of age-old pharisaism or hypocrisy. In no way, however, can this legitimate criticism become a justification for ignoring consideration of the character of the preacher. The person of the preacher is still and will always be the medium of the message. "The plain fact is that sermons, through the centuries, have had their greatest power when they have been preached by good men and women, people whose own lives quietly but surely mirrored the gospel of which they spoke."[23]

The autobiography of the preacher is never the subject of preaching, yet even at times when the message is lacking in logical development and the points are more diffused than focused, a personified message nonetheless comes through. James Russell Lowell's comment after hearing Ralph Waldo Emerson's Phi Beta Kappa address at Harvard in 1867 is illustrative. Lowell wrote, "Emerson's oration began nowhere and ended everywhere, and yet as always with that divine man, it left you feeling that something beautiful had passed that way—something more beautiful than anything else, like the rising and setting of the stars."[24] Although the preacher ought not to lean upon personal character and piety (as authentic as they may be) as a rationale for inadequate preparation, the most scholarly preparation can be undermined by an inauthentic human instrument.

Hunt's words are "preparing the preacher," by which he means the spiritual or moral formation of the preacher for the task of preaching. Hunt's instinctive Wesleyanism leads him correctly to speak of this as "holiness." Moreover, this concern is solidly grounded in Scripture: "This is the will of God, your sanctification" (1 Thess. 4:3 RSV); "Even as he chose us in him before the foundation of the world, that we should be holy and blameless before him" (Eph. 1:4 RSV); "As God's chosen ones, holy and beloved" (Col. 3:12*a* RSV).

As every Wesleyan knows, holiness of character depends upon the unfailing grace of Jesus Christ. A holy life is a grace-filled life. The emphasis on a character of holiness, Wesley held, was the distinctive gift God had given to the Methodists. The pardoning grace of Jesus Christ sets one free from all the compulsions for self-justification and delivers one from a preoccupation with oneself and its mistakenly claimed merits. A preacher justified by grace is one who is delivered from the idolatries of one's self-preoccupation, even the preoccupation with one's homiletical powers.

Freed from self-love, one is freed to live a new love—love for God and for one's neighbor. Wesley understood this to be the life of holiness or sanctification. Yet freedom from self-love is not a lawless freedom. The Christian is free, through the Holy Spirit, to live a life that faithfully fulfills God's moral law. In short, to live a life of love for God and for one's neighbor entails a blameless character. To be inattentive to the development of moral character and a life of piety is to ignore the Holy Spirit, for it is the Spirit's intention to form such moral character. The Spirit, however, is not willing to do this without human cooperation. Being inattentive to the development of moral character and a life of genuine piety leads to ignoring the neighbor's welfare whereby the pastor can become the neighbor's (or congregant's) "stumbling block."

If the preacher's charge is to tell the story of Jesus as God's salvation for us, the charge cannot be effectively fulfilled unless the story of God radiates from the preacher's own person. The offer of grace is the offer of a qualitatively different life. If this qualitatively new life in Christ is not evident in the preacher's character, the offer of grace through the preacher's words will have lost its sounding board.

Hunt's concern for the spiritual and moral life of the preacher was not a peripheral matter. It struck to the heart of the bishop's concern for preaching. "We have this treasure in earthen vessels," to be sure. But if the vessels are morally and spiritually flawed, the treasure may have to be carried in other vessels.

To stress the moral character of the preacher in such fashion is not to indulge in a moralism or legalism, old or new. That which the Spirit works to form within the pastor's person is, in Wesley's and Scripture's words, "the mind which was in Christ Jesus." Only then will the preacher's character become transparent to the character of Christ. Transparency to Christ is the objective of a holy character and is essential for an authentic speaking of the Word.

Hunt relates an incident following a preaching service that illustrates the transparency of character required for effective communication of the message. At the close of a service in which Bishop Hunt had preached, "a friend, superintendent of schools" in his home city, came down to the front of the church and handed him a slip of paper with three sentences written on it. Later Hunt read these words, "He stood before the cross and spoke; the people saw him, heard a voice but heeded not. He stood beside the cross and spoke; the people saw him and the cross, heard his voice, but heeded not. He stood behind the cross and spoke; the people saw not the preacher, but the cross, heard the voice of Jesus, and were saved."[25]

4. The Miracle of Preaching. Preaching, for Hunt, is more than scholarship and technique. When the preacher mounts the stairs to the sacred desk and begins to speak mere human words, a miracle can take place. The preparation for preaching, including wrestling with God in prayer, struggling over the scriptural

text, consulting the commentaries, and carefully crafting the sermon, can suddenly be transformed by the Spirit. In such a miraculous moment the words can become Word. Sensitive interpreters have called this an epiphany—an experience of an encounter with the divine.

Over this the preacher has no control. The preacher may earnestly desire it and pray for it, but the preacher cannot contrive an epiphany. Hunt relates such an epiphanous experience when for the first time he heard the Scottish divine James S. Stewart preach:

> The great Scotsman became so enthralled with his message, so recklessly eager to make its meaning and challenge clear to those of us listening that he suddenly began to pound the pulpit like an old-time country preacher. He left sentences trailing off in mid-air, unfinished, as he rushed on to others that clamored to be spoken. The gospel he was proclaiming consumed him, and the fires in his own soul set ours aflame. This is preaching, but it can only happen when a careful craftsman has mastered all the rules and been mastered by them, so that his preacher's soul may safely take flight and the winds of the Spirit catch and carry the gospel truth into the hearts of worshippers.[26]

Hunt was convinced that preaching begins and ends with God. First, God in Israel and in Christ has spoken. Through the Holy Spirit, God continues to speak by calling preachers and then inspiring their work. When the labors of preparation for preaching are finished and the preacher begins to speak, God once again speaks through the human words of the preacher. This is no resort, on the part of the preacher, to the Holy Spirit as a labor-saving device. Only the one who has endeavored to be a faithful steward of the Word, "rightly dividing the word of truth," has the right to believe this.

Somewhat like the Calvinist doctrine of the inspiration of Scripture (the Spirit inspired the writing of Scripture, and the same Spirit inspires the reception of the scriptural message) is the event of preaching in the church. This is the mystery with which Paul struggles. When the world by its wisdom knows not God, "it pleased God by the foolishness of preaching."

So strongly does Hunt believe that the preached Word calls and gathers the church, imbues its life with grace, and makes it bold to proclaim the gospel in the world, he finds it incredible that pastors should doubt its power or neglect its disciplines. The unimaginable joy of ministry is rooted in and flows from the grace-given privilege of "saying a good word for Jesus." At times he was profoundly perplexed that so many pastors could not grasp his vision. At other times he was particularly grateful when young pastors caught the contagious enthusiasm for preaching. He detected that new life came into their ministries, and even what was more important, new life came into the church.

The bishop never fancied himself a theorist of the art of preaching. He was content to be the practitioner. If itinerant ministry means traveling ministry (even for those of the episcopal office), which in the Wesleyan tradition indeed it does mean, Hunt was the proverbial circuit rider, traveling circuits without geographical boundaries. During his years of active episcopacy, he was featured in the 67th, 68th, 70th, and 72nd seasons of the Chicago Sunday Evening Club, a televised preaching forum originating from the Chicago Temple. Twice he was invited by the Keswick movement of Canada to preach for annual gatherings. Many times he was the preacher for services at the well-known Ocean Grove (New Jersey) campgrounds, and twice he preached for the annual Ocean Grove Camp Meeting. From the Presbyterians came the call to the Annual Ministers' Week at Massenetta Springs, Virginia. Across the span of years he preached in more than three hundred preaching missions in various parts of the United States. Across the United Methodist connection the bishop has preached in local churches large and small. He is a bishop who has taken itinerant preaching to be a fundamental component of the episcopal office.

"When he rises up in the pulpit," begins Leidig's musings on hearing Bishop Hunt preach, "all is made ready to turn the earth." The very physical presence of Hunt is almost magisterial. He towers over the pulpit. Then he begins to speak. His cadence is carefully timed to match the logic of his message. His words are chosen with literary sensitivity. His occasional quotations from his favorite Scottish preachers are exactly to the point. His adverbial modifiers to his adjectives—"*abstractly* theological," "*innocently* literary," "*rarely probingly* personal"—heighten the urgency of his appeal. Few can employ adverbs with such skill. His gestures are sparing. The communicative power lies in his words. Yet, as some Floridians have observed, when he stretches his arms across his chest, he is ready to preach. Everything else has been preliminary. Then the text shudders "through a giant presence."

Chapter Seven

❦

Evangelist

The Sulphur Springs camp meetings of his childhood, the annual revivals at First Church, Johnson City, in his youth, and the monthly youth rallies sponsored by the Johnson City Youth Council were formative influences in Earl Hunt's life that he never forgot. Evangelism as witness to the grace of God in Jesus Christ and invitation to a Spirit-endowed life of discipleship was almost "first nature" with him long before he entered the pastoral ministry. In his theological reflection he knew that evangelism was not an exercise in nostalgic memory but that the evangelical imperative was implicit in the gospel itself. The gospel was a story too good not to be true, and if so, it was a story too good not to be told. Grace was not a commodity to be dispensed but a new relationship with God through Christ to be lived and shared. Grace not shared was grace forfeited.

Theologically, Christ is the center of the Christian faith. From another perspective, experientially, the new relationship with God through Christ is the center. These, however, are not two centers. Rather, the juncture point between Christ and the life experience of the person is the one integral center. The evangelical witness arises from this integral center of Christ's saving action in the life of the believer. While everything the church does is not explicitly evangelism, everything the church does is permeated from this center. Christ the center is the irreducible rationale for the total ministry and mission of the church. For Hunt there is never an "appropriate time" for evangelism. All time is evangelistic time. Now, in every time and place, is the "hour of salvation."

In less than one year after retiring and moving back to the hills and mountains of North Carolina, Hunt was called from his Lake Junaluska home to Dallas at the urging of the Search Committee of The Foundation for Evangelism. Dr. Charles E. Kinder, who had been president of the foundation since 1979, had announced his resignation and was planning to resume his pastoral ministry in Florida, his home conference.

Dr. John H. Marshall Jr., noted geologist and petroleum specialist of Dallas, was the chairperson of both the foundation and the Search Committee. The Search Committee sought to persuade Hunt, who had recovered from his recent illness, to become the interim president of the foundation, effective July 1, 1989. Eventually, Marshall and his committee were sufficiently persuasive to secure Hunt's agreement for an interim period. In this case interim took on a strange definition. In 1990 Hunt assumed the full presidency and continued in that position until retirement in 1996. For one who had pursued a vigorous regimen of episcopal responsibilities for twenty-four years and had recently experienced serious health problems, it was even stranger that Hunt should emerge from retirement and assume new responsibilities that would be even more time and energy consuming than his former episcopal duties. For him the matter was quite simple: his church was calling.

The Foundation for Evangelism was founded in 1949 through the initiative of Harry Denman, a remarkable layman chronicled and fabled in Methodist annals. Denman, an Alabamian, had headed the General Board of Evangelism of The Methodist Church since the union of 1939. In the early days of the board, money was tight, as was the case in virtually all quarters of the church and the society. In fact, all the World Service money received by the General Board of Evangelism in a whole year was not sufficient to send a one-cent postcard to each Methodist!

The board was largely dependent upon all the outside financial help it could find. For this reason the General Board of Evangelism chartered The Foundation for Evangelism "to encourage persons and business organizations, whether individuals, partnerships or corporations; charitable funds and foundations and trusts; and all others to evidence their interest in the cause of evangelism by assisting in the financial support thereof." Further, the foundation was charged "to enlarge and extend the effectiveness of the program and work of the General Board of Evangelism of The Methodist Church beyond that now provided for by funds now available to it."[1]

Under the new organizational structures of The United Methodist Church of 1972, the foundation existed as an affiliate of the General Board of Discipleship with its own board of trustees. From 1979 until 1989 Charles Kinder served as the foundation's president. One project of the foundation during these years was the "Discover God's Call" program under the leadership of a layman, M. O. (Gus) Gustafson. Through retreats and weekend emphases in local churches this program was designed to assist laypeople in discerning their gifts and ways in which their gifts could be used in reaching out to unchurched people. Other programs during this same period included the biennial Denman Lectures, the annual conference Denman Awards, and the publication of *Forward,* an evangelism journal for The United Methodist Church.

By far the most ambitious undertaking of the foundation had been to secure the funding necessary to underwrite professorships of evangelism in United Methodist seminaries. The chairs were appropriately named in honor of the late E. Stanley Jones, missionary, evangelist, ecumenist extraordinaire. Under Kinder's leadership, chairs of evangelism were established at Boston University School of Theology and Garrett-Evangelical Theological Seminary, the two oldest theological schools in American Methodism. Kinder had also secured a generous financial commitment from Mr. and Mrs. B. B. Lane of Alta Vista, Virginia, which was earmarked for a position at Wesley Theological Seminary in the nation's capital, and preliminary conversations were under way with the seminary's administrators and faculty. The idea of establishing and underwriting chairs of evangelism in the United Methodist theological schools was one of Kinder's most creative ventures.[2]

In 1989 a controversy, covered widely by the church press, erupted involving a possible new professorship at Iliff School of Theology in Denver. The Iliff faculty had selected Mortimer Arias, a former president of the Latin American Biblical Seminary in San José, Costa Rica, and a former bishop of the Methodist Church in Bolivia, as its choice to fill the post. Arias had served as a member of the World Council of Churches' Commission on World Mission and Evangelism and as professor of Hispanic studies and evangelization at the School of Theology, Claremont, California. In 1984 Arias had authored the book *Announcing the Reign of God: Evangelization and the Subversive Memory of Jesus,* which had been favorably reviewed by such evangelical scholars as Harvie M. Conn of Westminster Theology Seminary and Mark Branson, dean of Fellowship Bible Institute.[3]

The final agreement between the foundation and Iliff had not been settled when the faculty selection was announced. Kinder would not agree to the appointment. Iliff's interpretation of the ensuing problem focused on issues of academic freedom, and that side of the story caught the attention of the press. Other United Methodist seminaries were considering the possibility of an evangelism addition to their faculties. Considerable confusion arose in the church. The foundation did not have a clearly phrased policy statement outlining the guidelines and procedures for such appointments. Misunderstandings and missteps occurred on all sides of the issue. Kinder, for personal reasons, including a serious health problem, submitted his resignation and accepted an appointment in Sebring, Florida, offered by Bishop Hasbrouck Hughes.

The Search Committee of the foundation was seeking an interim president who could pilot them through, keeping the professorship program going and building a collegial relationship with the theological schools. That was why the Search Committee had brought Hunt to Dallas. In the eyes of the committee Hunt was the most qualified person in the church. The Hunts were settled in their retirement home at Lake Junaluska, which happened to be the headquarters of the foundation. Hunt had accrued valuable years of experience as a college president. He understood the academic community. He had wide visibility in the connectional church. His commitments to evangelism were beyond question. His credentials matched the job definition perfectly. A friend and retired episcopal colleague has stated that Hunt was indeed "the right person, at the right time, and in the right place."

On July 1, 1989, Hunt assumed the responsibilities of interim president. His academic experience prompted him to address immediately the issue of guidelines and principles governing the relationship of the foundation to the theological schools. He composed a three-page single-spaced draft, which he sent to Dr. Douglass Lewis, president of Wesley Theological Seminary in

Washington, D.C. Lewis was an experienced academic administrator and was sympathetic to the foundation's program of professorships.

In the late fall of 1989, Hunt met with Lewis and a faculty member of Wesley Seminary. The three hammered out the principles statement, which was then circulated among the foundation's board members and selected academic administrators including Deans James Waites of Candler and Dennis Campbell of Duke. In January 1990 the foundation's board unanimously approved the statement of principles safeguarding the rights and responsibilities of both the foundation and the theological schools.

In October 1989 the foundation celebrated the fortieth anniversary of its founding with a banquet at the Lambuth Inn at Lake Junaluska. Hunt, with his intuitive sense of timing and his fondness for the ceremonial, claimed the occasion for renewing a positive image of the foundation before the church.

First, at the banquet the foundation affirmed its historical continuity by paying special tribute to Dr. Kinder for his ten years of leadership. His most notable achievement had been the creation of the E. Stanley Jones Professorships in the United Methodist theological institutions. Already the positions at Boston and Garrett were in place, and the possibility of a new position at Wesley was under consideration. As yet the chairs were not underwritten with endowment. Kinder had crossed the church raising the funds for the annual support of the professorships. The foundation was keenly appreciative of his labors. Those in attendance were familiar with the history of the foundation and were aware that the vision of Harry Denman for the foundation and its work would probably not have survived had it not been for the labors and leadership of Kinder and his wife, Phyllis. Dr. Marshall, the chair of the foundation's board, presented Kinder with the Denman Evangelism Award, expressing the board's gratitude for all he had given to the foundation through his "prayers, gifts, and service."

Next, the foundation affirmed its commitment to the project of the professorships in the theological schools. The commitment was symbolically represented by the major speaker of the evening, Dr. Neal F. Fisher, president of Garrett-Evangelical Theological Seminary, where the second professorship was already a reality with Dr. Robert G. Tuttle Jr. as occupant of the chair.

In commemorating the forty years of the foundation's life, a unique feature of the banquet program was the recognition of Forty Distinguished Evangelists of the Methodist world whose lives and careers overlapped either wholly or partially the period in which the foundation had been in existence. The list of honorees was broadly inclusive: Mary McLeod Bethune (1875–1955), African American educator; John Calvin Broomfield (1872–1950), a former Methodist Protestant pastor and one of the first two bishops elected from his branch of the church in 1939; Violetta Cavallero (1912–1988), a dedicated pastor in Montevideo; Bishop Ralph Spaulding Cushman (1879–1960), who was chairperson of the Commission on Evangelism prior to the formation of the General Board of Evangelism in 1939; Harry Denman (1893–1976), founder of the foundation; Dr. James Walter Golden (1883–1968), associate general secretary of the Board of Evangelism in 1944 and father of Bishop Charles F. Golden; E. Stanley Jones (1884–1973), who once declined his election to the episcopacy to continue his missionary evangelistic ministry in India; Helen Kim (1899–1970), who had served as president of Ewha University in Korea; John R. Mott (1865–1955), one of the founders of the Student Volunteer Movement and the World Council of Churches and Nobel laureate; Daniel Thambyrajah Niles (1908–1970), famed

Sri Lankan minister and a member of the Presidium of the World Council of Churches; George H. Outen (1921–1980), general secretary of the General Board of Church and Society and called by some "a Holy Ghost preacher"; Albert C. Outler (1908–1989), eminent Wesleyan scholar and ecumenist; Earl Arnette Seamands (1891–1984), named Missionary of the Century by the South India Annual Conference in 1976; Mortimer Arias (1924–), a former bishop of the Methodist Church in Bolivia; Emilio Castro (1927–), general secretary of the World Council of Churches; Donald English (1930–1998), twice elected president of the British Methodist Conference; John Ed Matheson (1936–), pastor of Frazer Memorial United Methodist Church, Montgomery, the fastest growing church in the denomination; and Alan Walker (1911–), director of World Evangelism of the World Methodist Council from 1978 to 1981, who had been knighted by Queen Elizabeth; and the list went on. Forty years and forty evangelists! An expansive and richly textured roster of Methodists from home and around the world brought to life the late Halford Luccock's description of Methodist history—"an endless line of splendor!"

For Hunt 1989 was preliminary to the demanding tasks ahead. Beginning in 1990 the foundation initiated the Evangelist of the Year award, singling out for recognition each year a United Methodist who modeled for the church the ministry of evangelism. Recipients are chosen by a committee external to the board that receives nominations from across the church and selects one to be honored at the annual meeting of the board. Recipients have included Dr. Joe Harding, Dr. Malone Dodson, Dr. James Buskirk, Bishop Kenneth Carder, Dr. Eddie Fox, Dr. Kirby John Caldwell, Dr. James Barnes, and the Reverend Stephen Rhodes.

In 1991 another new feature of the foundation was announced

when Dr. Ralph W. Mohney was designated as the Distinguished Evangelist in Residence at the General Board of Discipleship in Nashville. Dr. Mohney came to the new position after having served distinguished pastorates in the Holston Conference and was a former president of Tennessee Wesleyan College, one of Holston's institutions of higher education. Mohney and Hunt had been close friends for many years and shared common commitments to evangelism and higher education.

From his constant reading of biography Hunt knew the importance of historical consciousness. When the time came for the 1993 annual meeting of the board of the foundation, the occasion marked the centennial of the birth of Harry Denman. This legendary figure had died in 1976, but Denman would never have called it that. His word for dying was coronation! Friends and supporters joined the foundation's board in Nashville to memorialize the life of Denman and to celebrate the advances of the foundation over the forty-four years of its life since Denman had founded it.

The foundation had already established professorships at Boston and Garrett, and the board could now report two additional professorships. At Wesley Theological Seminary the faculty had in January 1990 elected James C. Logan to fill the new position. Logan, the senior member of the faculty, had for twenty-five years held a position in systematic theology and had been active in the Virginia Conference and the General Conferences of the church. In 1993 Saint Paul School of Theology called Dr. Harold Knight to fill its new post. Knight, a Wesleyan scholar and the author of a study of John Wesley and the means of grace, was recognized as a rising young evangelical voice. Other professorship possibilities were looming on the horizon. Hunt was already in conversation with Dean Dennis Campbell of Duke. The professorship program was obviously gaining momentum.

What better way to remember Harry Denman than to expand the work of the foundation? Denman was remembered at the Nashville program with the announcement that *Harry Denman: A Biography*, written by Harold Rogers in 1977, had been reissued with the financial support of the foundation.[4] A new volume, *Prophetic Evangelist—The Living Legacy of Harry Denman*,[5] a joint effort of the foundation and the General Board of Discipleship, was announced with Ezra Earl Jones, general secretary of the Board of Discipleship, and Phillip Connolly, representative of the foundation, making the presentation. Harry Denman, whom Billy Graham once called "the greatest practitioner of personal evangelism in America," had left a legacy that the foundation sought not only to remember but also to continue.

The administrative responsibilities of the foundation continued to grow. Hunt was speaking widely throughout the church and making valuable contacts for the financial support of the professorships. But he needed assistance. In 1992 Dr. Curtis Schofield, pastor and former president of Hiwassee College in the Holston Conference, came to the foundation as vice president for development. Schofield conceived of a new program called AC-70 in which annual conferences became support agents for the foundation by contributing $1,000 or more, one-half of which was returned to support evangelistic work in the donor conferences. Soon Northwest Texas, Holston, West Ohio, and North Georgia Conferences had entered this relationship with the foundation.

Hunt set in place an Advisory Council made up of twenty-two pastors and laypersons who would meet with him periodically to convey input from the grassroots and to advise the president on program plans of the foundation. In addition, a system of regional directors was created. These persons serve as advocates for the foundation and assist in cultivating their geographical areas for its support.

Hunt also developed a system of staff ministers, United Methodist clergy who could be called upon by the foundation for a variety of services. Dr. Ben St. Clair was Hunt's first executive assistant in this program, and St. Clair, a fund-raiser of the first order, cultivated more than one million dollars for the support of the foundation. Dr. James R. Crook, retired Florida Conference district superintendent and resident at Lake Junaluska, succeeded St. Clair. Crook has been assisted by Bishop Monk Bryan, retired bishop of the South Central Jurisdiction; Dr. Joe A. Harding, Corvallis, Oregon; Dr. William R. Key, Perry, Georgia; Dr. Joseph E. Taylor, Fayetteville, Arkansas; and Dr. Charles G. Turkington, Lake Junaluska.

Hunt had from the beginning of his ministry been convinced that evangelism was methodologically a matter of heart and mind, affection and cognition, rigorous reflection and committed practice. He knew his Wesleyan tradition well enough to embrace fully its conjunctive character of faith and reason, conversion and nurture, faith and works.

Sensing how easily evangelism can slip into a mind-set of technique without theological substance, he summoned more than fifty Methodist scholars and leaders to the symposium "Theology and Evangelism in the Wesleyan Heritage," held on the campus of Emory University, February 5-9, 1992. The event, which was conceived, developed, and funded solely by the foundation, was the most sharply focused undertaking in the arena of theological thought and evangelistic mission ever attempted by the foundation, and perhaps by any agency of United Methodism. The participants grappled seriously and intentionally with both the long-range and the near-at-hand biblical and theological issues related to the recovery of evangelistic urgency in the church.

The participants represented the continents of Africa, Asia, Europe, and North and South America and included ten bishops, one former bishop, one who would be elected to the episcopacy five months later, one university president, three heads of theological institutions, twelve seminary professors, six pastors, four connectional leaders, one district superintendent, and the general secretary of the World Methodist Council. The papers from this symposium were edited and published in 1994,[6] and the foundation provided boxed and labeled sets of the fifteen color videocassette recordings of the twelve major presentations and responses, which were distributed to appropriate institutions and agencies of the church. The scholarly quality of the symposium and the subsequent publication of the anthology furthered academic and intellectual respect for evangelism within the church and, even more important, within the theological schools.

No sooner had the news of this symposium been reported in the church press than Hunt was busy at the drafting board again. Whereas the first symposium had been focused more toward the theological schools, the new symposium was to be centered on the internal life of the church itself. This time the episcopal leadership of the church was asked to assume the principal responsibilities.

On March 9-12, 1995, nineteen bishops of The United Methodist Church were joined by more than 150 other persons in the Oxnam Chapel of Wesley Theological Seminary in Washington. Bishops presenting papers were Neil L. Irons, R. Sheldon Duecker, George W. Bashore, Ann B. Sherer, Richard B. Wilke, Bruce P. Blake, Hae-Jong Kim, Elias G. Galvan, Ruediger R. Minor, Woodie W. White, Kenneth L. Carder, Alfred L. Norris, Arthur F. Kulah, David J. Lawson, and James K. Mathews with Bishop Joseph H. Yeakel preaching for the closing service of worship on Sunday morning in Metropolitan Memorial United Methodist Church. A fifty-voice choir of the Korean United Methodist Church of Greater Washington sang, and the Reverend Stephen Rhodes and other leaders of Culmore United Methodist Church, Falls Church, Virginia, presented an experimental program on multicultural evangelism. Bishop and Mrs. Edwin C. Boulton led all the services of worship.

In reflecting upon the symposium, Bishop Hunt commented: "I believe the Washington Consultation was the only occasion during my lifetime when the episcopal leadership of our denomination has been afforded a forum to deal exclusively with the theme of Christian evangelism." The papers presented were edited and published in 1996 under the title *Christ for the World: United Methodist Bishops Speak on Evangelism.*[7] The Sunday edition of *The Washington Times* carried a full front-page report of the symposium.

Bishop Hunt brought to the foundation his personal commitment, perceptive analyses of the church, administrative abilities, and a commanding voice within the church. When he retired from the presidency in 1996, he could count six new professorships of evangelism in the schools of theology: Wesley Theological Seminary, Saint Paul School of Theology, Duke University Divinity School, the Methodist Theological School in Ohio, the Evangelisch-Methodistische Kirche Theologisches Seminar in Reutlingen, Germany, and the Africa University in Harare, Zimbabwe. He could also report the full endowment of one chair. Other schools were lining up before the foundation's doors.

In 1995 Paul R. Ervin Jr., an attorney from Atlanta, came to the foundation as executive vice president to give Hunt much needed assistance in dealing with the unusually heavy demands that now characterized the foundation's work and program. He had served as the conference lay leader and chancellor of the North Georgia Conference and had been president of the National Association of Annual Conference Lay Leaders.

When Bishop Hunt announced his retirement date of 1996, the foundation was at the point of its greatest strength and could claim an expansive outreach unequaled in its history. Would Harry Denman recognize his foundation today? Perhaps not. It has grown beyond his dreams of forty-six years ago. He would nevertheless welcome the advances the foundation has made, and he would applaud a bishop who came out of retirement to make his dream come true.

An account of Hunt's more than seven years with the foundation could give the mistaken impression that he is primarily a strategist for evangelism. To the contrary, Earl Hunt is an evangelist! He has been a practitioner of the evangelism that he espouses. Furthermore, for years he has been deeply concerned that evangelism recover its intellectual and theological integrity.

His biographical reading of Jonathan Edwards, the leading figure of the First Great Awakening, and Charles Grandison Finney, who is credited with being the father of American revivalism, has convinced him that there is "no contradiction between faith and reason, or between zealous soul-winning and unapologetic intellectual integrity."[8] A valid evangelism must rest upon the foundation of sound biblical interpretation and theological understanding. In 1938 one of Hunt's favorite episcopal figures, Edwin Holt Hughes, after commenting about Jonathan Edwards and Charles Finney, asked if it could be possible that "someday we shall see that conjunction again—the mighty evangelist represented in the eminent educator?" After all, in the figures of John Wesley and Saint Paul we find that "the real scholar and the flaming preacher have more than once dwelt in a single personality."[9]

Hunt's Denman Lectures of 1994, *Evangelism for a New Century*,[10] along with his sermons, provide a reliable basis from which to derive an overall view of his understanding of evangelism. Hunt demonstrates that he, an evangelist, is simultaneously the thinker combining the passions of the heart with the rational acumen of a theological mind. Few are more widely read in theology and the practice of evangelism than he, and few are more intuitively perceptive. He knows where he stands, and more important, he knows why.

Hunt's conceptual grasp of evangelism is decidedly a proclamation model, though he has never sought to classify his position. Evangelism is first and always a declaration of God's gracious and salvific turning toward the human race in Jesus Christ. The revelatory and saving event of Jesus Christ is the source and definition of evangelism. In a proclamation model, evangelism is defined by the message of what God has done and is doing, rather than by methods and strategies. All other considerations are subordinated to the message, and the message determines the appropriateness of all other considerations.

"Getting the message straight before getting it out" is primary. And what is the message? The message concentrates with single-mindedness upon its subject—God's saving revelation in Jesus Christ. In short, the focus of the message is not oneself or even the church. Human biography or personal experience, social circumstances, and events of the time have their place, but none of these in themselves is the topic of evangelistic proclamation. The message is focused upon the incarnate Christ and his atoning death and resurrection as the decisive and determinative events of eschatological salvation.

Proclamation Evangelism is quite simply "naming the name" of Jesus. The first and unqualified responsibility of one who witnesses is to be faithful to the Evangel, the good news of Jesus

Christ. From the very beginning the message is good news of what God has done. On occasion Hunt quotes Joseph Fort Newton, "He entered into the soul of humanity like a dye, the tinge of which no acid can remove."[11] Objectively, God has acted in Christ. This world with all of its ambiguity and godforsaken-ness has been claimed by God's grace in Christ. A stable in Bethlehem, a cross on Calvary, and an empty tomb in a Jerusalem garden are God's story of at-one-ment, and the invitation of evangelism is extended to all who in faith will enter into God's story. Something new has happened in Bethlehem and Jerusalem! God has done a "new thing."

The first obligation of the church as a witnessing people is to proclaim the wondrous story of Jesus and his love. Bethlehem, Calvary, and Jerusalem are not mere geographical locations. Together they are the gospel story. Incarnation, Atonement, and Resurrection are the chapters making up the one story that is Jesus Christ. "The Incarnation," preached Hunt, "reminds us again and afresh that God has betrothed Himself forever to humanity!" The Cross—"this is our message—not the dialectic of human philosophy—but Jesus Christ and Him crucified: forgiveness of sin, redemption for lost and lonely mankind!" And the Resurrection—"the triumphant concluding clause in God's great sentence to humankind." Hunt's conclusion is, "This—and only this—is the foundation for our message about both personal and social religion."[12]

Get the message straight! Then, and only then, get the message out. As important as strategies and methods are, they must always be in service to the message and consonant with the message. A proclamation model is not confined to the specific function of preaching, though preaching is paradigmatic for the model. A proclamation model is fixed upon the message; its communication may be in various forms and styles. The message, however, is both source and norm for the whole process of evangelism.

Although there are others who take a more dialogic view of evangelism, beginning with the questions of human existence and seeking to correlate the theological answers, Hunt takes another tack. He is no Tillichian! Rather than existence focusing its questions upon the gospel, the gospel defines existence and its questions. Hunt seems to eschew any apologetic shaping of the message to fit a predefined human condition. The gospel defines sin, not sin the gospel. On one occasion, Hunt wrote, "Our departure from an emphasis upon the reality of God . . . is traceable not so much to a new psychology as it is to a diluted theology. We have not been that sure of God Himself! . . . Shame on us for trying to alter the nature of God to fit our little philosophical presuppositions."[13]

Others propose a nurture or spiritual formation model for evangelism. Ben Campbell Johnson writes, "Instead of the proclaimer of the gospel . . . we suggest the spiritual guide, which is a softer, less aggressive model."[14] In Hunt's mind nurture certainly plays an important role in evangelism. How else could he position himself with his persistent advocacy of education and an intelligent presentation of the gospel? But Christian formation is subsequent to, not antecedent to, the proclamation. John Westerhoff once argued, "We can nurture persons into institutional religion, but not into mature Christian faith. The Christian faith by its very nature demands conversion."[15] Hunt would concur with this logic.

Proclamation Evangelism is telling the story of Jesus, which has the power to *convict*. Hunt's most frequently used words of the human condition are *lost, anxious*, and *disobedient*. The gospel reveals the condition of humankind as "sinful," yet a sinful race to which God has spoken the word of grace in Jesus

Christ. Lost, the human race resembles Kierkegaard's butterfly flitting from one blossom to another, never able to find the ultimate nectar. The human plight portrays symptoms of a deep, dreadful anxiety that threatens to freeze human beings into a paralysis of lethargy or send them into a frenzied chase for one fanciful but nebulous cultural god after another. In disobedience to the will and purpose of God, the human race indulges itself in self-defeating and self-destructing immorality. Whether the condition is dislocation or lostness, anxiety or spiritual dementia, moral disobedience or indifference, the grace of Christ reveals both God's inviolable holiness against our sin and God's limitless mercy for us. The story of Jesus has the power to convict human beings whose paradoxical condition is that of living without God and yet nevertheless living before God.

Hunt is instructed by his Wesleyan tradition to call this the working of prevenient grace. The grace of Christ "goes before us" to awaken us and to lead us to repentance. In short, the first work of the grace of Christ is to convict. This same grace of Christ leads us to the experience of conversion where life is fundamentally changed from "lost" to "found," from "anxiety" to "assurance," and from "disobedience" to "submission." The linkage of "from" and "to" is the work of the Holy Spirit in effecting new birth, changed by the grace of Christ from the "conviction of sin" to the "conviction of Christ."

The message of new birth suffers at two hands today. The doctrine of the new birth suffers from silence in many established churches. On the other hand, in popularized Christianity new birth is often treated as a "terminal" point rather than a "beginning" point in one's life of faith. New birth is actually the intersection point where God's action in Christ meets the human condition of separation from God. In Wesleyan terms the new birth is the connecting point between justification (the forgiveness of sin) and sanctification (the empowerment to live a new life of love for God and for the neighbor). In short, new birth is the beginning of a radically changed life.

If the preacher is serious about evangelism, the goal of which is changed lives, then the preacher should carefully examine the content and rhetoric of her or his sermons.

> Too many times sermons can prove to be exciting intellectual encounters with intriguing ideas, even ideas about the Bible, lofty philosophical monologues in which the holy, transforming presence of the living, loving, compassionate Lord is totally missing. There is no burning bush, no cry from Calvary, and there are rarely changed lives in the wake of such preaching.[16]

Proclamation Evangelism aims toward the goal of *restoration* of human life. Hunt is theologically modest in attempting to define the atoning death of Christ in the form of a theory. The Atonement is not a proposition or idea; it is the divine act of forgiveness or restoration of a broken humanity. Rather than creating a neat and concise theory, Hunt—the proclaimer—draws upon the wealth of biblical metaphors to speak of salvation, redemption, justification, and reconciliation. Grace is the key metaphor, holding all the others in a cohesive whole. By the grace of Christ we have a new standing before God and a new relationship with God. By the grace of Christ we have a new location within the community of God, the church. By the grace of Christ we have a new life to live and a new calling to fulfill. Such is possible only if human life is restored. This is precisely the summary work of Jesus Christ, which can best be described as restoration or homecoming, Hunt repeatedly draws upon G. K. Chesterton's "The House of Christmas" to describe the restoring grace of Christ:

To an open house in the evening
Home shall men come,
To an older place than Eden
And a taller town than Rome.
To the end of the way of the wandering star,
To the things that cannot be and that are,
To the place where God was homeless
And all men are at home.[17]

Hunt's passion for preaching and equally his passion for evangelism are fused in his understanding of evangelism as proclamation. "Vital evangelism should always eventuate in discipling," Hunt declared in 1997, "but it is forever the Holy Spirit's work, and the achievement is God's achievement. Our task is to provide the witness."[18]

Nowhere in all of Bishop Hunt's books and sermons do we find evangelism treated as systematically as in the Denman Lectures. He maps out the contours of the contemporary culture, which he characterizes as "the arena of problems," the fundamental problem being that "our hearers are not in any condition to receive our message: the pattern, culture, temper, and climate of their lives are set in a secular field."[19] The climate within the church is no less acute than in the general culture. He agrees with the analysis of Professor Leander Keck who, in the Lyman Beecher Lectures of 1992, summarizes the situation: "To be sure the mainliners have not repudiated evangelism: they have simply put it on the back burner . . . [or] to shift metaphors, the fires of evangelistic commitment have been banked for the duration."[20] Hunt is not content to remain with analysis; he sees the fundamental problem to be existential. Whether people are conscious of it, there is a deep, haunting need for something or someone outside ourselves, the "human need for a Savior."[21] If the church is to rise to meet this contemporary need, the church will have to recover the story or gospel that has been entrusted to it. True to the heart of his proclamation model of evangelism, Hunt returns in the Denman Lectures to the theological content of proclamation or witness. Without a renewal or recovery of the biblical/theological message of a "seeking God and the wonder of the cross on Golgotha,"[22] all efforts at strategy will be empty and futile. Within the scope of four short, readable lectures Hunt presented a concise analysis of the culture, a theology of the evangelistic witness, and some concrete prescriptions for the contemporary church.

The judgment of many persons is that Hunt's lectures have not received the attention that they merit. This may be due, in part, to a matter that arose in the course of his delivery of the lectures. For a stretch of months in late 1993 and early 1994 the church's heated attention was fixed upon an ecumenical conference of church women, "The Re-Imagining Conference," held in Minneapolis in November 1993. Hunt viewed with alarm reports carried by the press of some addresses at the conference. He considered much of the contemporary speculation about the notion of Sophia to be unbiblical and heretical. He plainly called the speculation "heresy" in both spoken and written word. Soon he was at the center of the controversy sweeping across the church. While his criticism was unequivocal, it contained more biblical and theological sophistication than most of the responses to the conference. One and a half pages of closely argued footnotes reveal the seriousness with which he viewed the matter.[23] Consequently, however, the Denman Lectures of 1994 are remembered more for the Sophia controversy than for their concise systematic treatment of evangelism in the contemporary church and world.

From the time of his sermon for the inauguration of the new

professorship at Wesley Theological Seminary in 1990, to the Denman Lectures in 1994, to his article "The Right Kind of Evangelism" in *Circuit Rider* in 1997, Hunt has focused on two theological developments on the contemporary scene that threaten the Christian witness: "a widespread impact from religious syncretism and theological universalism."[24]

The "religious syncretism" to which he refers is seen in recent efforts to develop a "theology of religion" in which Christianity is viewed as but one way among other religious confessions. Actually, this development is as old as the nineteenth century, when Ernst Troeltsch, smitten by the methods of historicism, claimed that all religions are relative. Any claim to absoluteness had to be radically qualified.

Hunt's analytical eye is focused upon a new awareness of the religious pluralism of the global world. Where once Westerners could point to "over there" when talking about the "religions," the presence of the "religions" is now seen every day in our shopping malls and along our streets. The proximity of the "religions" presents a new factor in the context of evangelistic witness in a new time.

Rather than repeatedly pointing to the proponents of a theological relativism, Hunt could point to and draw upon an increasing volume of writing that counters these relativistic claims. Only once does he cite a countering voice: William Abraham's notion of the "Cosmic Christ."[25] Hunt has always been good at ringing the alarms, and this is important. From his Emory and Henry days one colleague recalls that he could anticipate the crisis and "head off" its occurrence. A cabinet member in one of his areas remarked good-naturedly that every cabinet meeting had a "crisis." In the case of the challenge of religious pluralism the crisis is real and manifests itself in the form of a pervasive, naive relativism that saturates the popular culture.

There is a need to ring the bell, but there is a need also to sound the trumpet!

Universalism or universal salvation is a doctrine that has been around as long as Origen (c. A.D. 185–254). To some, universalism is particularly persuasive on the current scene as a way to reconcile the problem of evil and to answer the question about those who have never heard the gospel. Again, Hunt is on target in sensing the implications of this thought for evangelism. Religious pluralism and universalism can easily be combined in a rhetorical argument numbing the nerve of Christian witness.

Hunt juxtaposes another kind of universalism that he has learned from the Wesleyan tradition. The Methodists have long sung Charles's words, "Pure universal love thou art!" From the time of John Wesley, the Methodists have held that universal grace is accessible and available to all. The one necessary condition is faith. This has been the conviction firing the zeal of Methodists in their higher moments. An evangelism worthy of the name of Wesley should never tire of singing, "O that the world might taste and see the riches of his love."

Hunt clearly espouses the Wesleyan doctrine of the free grace of Christ universally accessible to all people. He does not offer an internal critique of the doctrine of universal salvation about which he is alarmed. Nor does he offer a counterargument. He senses the critical issues involved and waits for the theologians of the church to respond.

Hunt, the evangelist, has been unrelenting across the years of his ministry of proclaiming "the measures of God's grace." He has been an administrator of evangelism, and he has dared to be the proclaimer. Since 1988 he has remarked on occasion that perhaps his greatest work in his episcopal years was his chairing of the Committee on Our Theological Task during the quadrennium of 1984–1988. As important as this work was, history may see otherwise. He may have offered in his retirement years a greater contribution to the church. At least, as with Harry Denman, he has seen to it that evangelism as integral to the church's life and mission is not debatable. We may debate how it is done, but we cannot debate that it should be done.

Chapter Eight

🍂

Educator

In the summer of 1956 a thirty-eight-year-old pastor arrived in Emory, Virginia, to become the fourteenth president of Emory and Henry College. Little in the pastoral ministry of Earl Hunt had prepared him for the responsibilities of his new post. His preaching abilities had attracted attention beyond the bounds of the Holston Conference. Yet the sacred desk and a president's desk had little in common. He had reared a congregation and built a new church sanctuary in Chattanooga, but raising a college budget was a very different matter. He had been chosen Young Man of the Year in Morristown, but measured in square feet Morristown could not compare with the territory to be cultivated to produce new support constituency for a college. The demands of pastoral ministry had not permitted sufficient time to study the history and philosophy of higher education, even the more limited scope of church-related education. Even if he had had time for such theoretical preparation, he had received no intimations that a college presidency was in his future. He was a pastor-preacher—and an effective one at that. But could he be an educator? That was the question.

From the time of his installation as president to his consecration as bishop, Hunt's almost single-minded focus became the ministry of Christian higher education. By the time of the dawning of the bright spring day of May 11, 1957, the day of his installation, he knew something of the vision of those early Methodist settlers of the valleys of southwestern Virginia and East Tennessee. He knew that their decision to found a college had not been their vision alone.

A few years before this action took place, the founding conference of The Methodist Episcopal Church in 1784 articulated the missional consciousness of the new church in the explicit words of John Wesley, "to spread scriptural holiness over the land." They were to ride the vast circuits preaching the news of salvation through Christ. They were to seize the institution of the camp meeting to bring the masses to Jesus. They also knew that "the spread of scriptural holiness" meant the penetration of the new republic with the "virtues of the King." For these reasons, that first conference voted to establish a college. From that day they were strongly committed to education as a primary way to "spread scriptural holiness." Even a circuit rider like Peter Cartwright, who at times derided an educated ministry, made a financial contribution toward the establishment of McKendree College.

The Methodists' ill-fated experience with the establishment of Cokesbury College (opened in 1787 and destroyed by fire in 1795) at Abingdon, Maryland, did not diminish their ardor for the mission of education. By 1836 the Methodists had established six educational institutions: Randolph Macon in Virginia (1830), Wesleyan University in Connecticut (1831), Dickinson in Pennsylvania (1834), two Georgia schools of Emory (1836) and Wesleyan (1836), and, yes, Emory and Henry (1836), the first such institution in frontier Methodism. The young church's primary concern in founding these institutions was to provide their children with an education in the arts, religion, and morals with which most of the older generation had not been blessed. Never absent from their considerations in establishing the colleges, however, had been a firm conviction that the welfare of "the soul of the nation" required such education. "In the United States," wrote Alexis de Tocqueville, "the influence of religion is not confined to the manners, but extends to the intelligence of the people."[1]

On the day of his installation Hunt knew that he was taking his place in a missional tradition that extended from the Holy Club of the Wesley brothers at Oxford through more than a century and a half of American Methodism. Charles Wesley had verbalized the vision in the words written for the reconstitution of the Kingswood School in 1748, "Unite the pair so long disjoined, knowledge and vital piety." From the beginning the Methodists had sensed that one expression of the mission of "scriptural holiness" was the uniting of knowledge and piety, mind and heart.

On that spring day the young president saw that the mission of a church-related college in uniting the two, mind and heart, required an unapologetic acknowledgment of and commitment to Jesus Christ. To what extent Hunt was aware in 1956 of the erosion of Christian identity in church-related colleges is difficult to assess. Certainly by the decades of 1940 and 1950, church-related colleges were defining their mission in less specific ways. A reading of the mission statements in the colleges' catalogs offers ample illustration. Increasingly, the colleges were expressing their religious and ecclesiastical commitments in broader and more general terms. For example, the church-related college existed to promote moral maturity in the individual, to foster the service motive toward the wider society, and to inculcate the values of personal integrity, respect for others, and love of learning. Or the institution's goal was to contribute to a common search for knowledge and to provide an atmosphere of caring for the individual student.

At exactly the time Hunt was assuming the presidency of a church-related college, the church's institutions, at least partly in response to the growing pluralism of the society, were fleeing the specifics of the Christian vocabulary and mouthing "values" more directly derived from Enlightenment mentality than from a denomination's confession of Christian faith. Embedded in Hunt's carefully sculptured words of his inaugural address were these:

> The old dichotomy between the culture of the mind and the conversion of the soul must be destroyed. The relevance of God and the redemptive process centering in Jesus Christ and His Person and work to the entire educational experience must be acknowledged with a candor and enthusiasm reminiscent of the great religious awakenings of the 18th and 19th centuries.[2]

The new president was aware that his commitment was congruent with the mind of the founders of the college. That this commitment was in tension with the more recent attempts to modify the older or to fashion a newer rationale for the church's engagement in higher education is unclear. What is transparently clear is that he knew what the original vision was—the uniting of mind and heart centered in the "redemptive process" of Jesus Christ and extending "to the entire educational experience." The subsequent years of his service to the church reveal that he remained steadfast in his conviction that no less than this was essential in maintaining a "recognizable" Christian institution.

In addition, Hunt was ready to enumerate the functional specifics of the mission of the church-related college, but such functions were derivatives of the principle of the union of the "redemptive process" and the "educational experience." The college, the academy of the church, existed to teach with integrity, communicating truth with accuracy, understanding, and challenge. Hunt knew that in the liberal arts curriculum there were no disciplines known as Christian biology or Christian calculus, as though the term *Christian* indicated a body of scientific knowledge. He knew that a Christian liberal arts curriculum demanded accuracy, which entailed academic freedom in the pursuit of that accuracy. He knew profoundly that while there was not an identifiable Christian curriculum, there was inescapably a Christian environment, namely, the church-related college, and there was the Christian teacher-scholar. In the church-related school there could be no compromise with academic excellence and academic freedom. Hunt pressed his point, "Identification with high religious principle is incentive for excellence rather than excuse for mediocrity in matters of academic standards."[3]

An educational institution committed to Jesus Christ is without qualification committed to values derived from Jesus Christ and absolutely necessary for the living of the Christian life. The church-related college cannot be content merely with perfunctory religious emphasis weeks and required chapel attendance. Although these have their place, they cannot in and of themselves "stem the tide of moral irresponsibility whose cynical waters lash dangerously at the lovely houses we have built on the sand."[4] What is required is a constructive effort to build up the total moral, ethical, and spiritual system of the college as a whole. "What is the permanent effect upon human personality," Hunt questioned, "of cheating in an examination? Is there a correlation between this regrettable practice and the eventual collapse of truth and honor in a young person's life? If so, the gradual disappearance of functioning honor systems in American institutions of higher learning has tragic relevance where the future of human freedom is concerned."[5]

The church-related college "ought to accept as one of its normal and fortunate responsibilities the training of professional and lay leadership for the Christian Church."[6] Here, in particular, the curriculum of religion plays a central role. A church-related college should offer the courses in Bible, church history, and Christian thought and ethics taught with the same academic rigor as any other academic discipline. The church-related college, however, ought not to be content to present the intellectual content of the faith simply as "comparative religious studies." In the church-related college such courses should be taught with academic integrity suffused with a deeper understanding born from an active involvement in Christian community, which confesses and practices the Christian faith.

At a time when many representatives of church-related institutions played down their church connections in order to attract a larger audience, Hunt was explicit, "The production of lay church leaders must not be a vague and peripheral purpose in the church-related institution's catalogue of objectives; it must be among its definite and central goals."[7] He was dealing with concrete issues of church-connectedness, which lay and clergy of the conference could easily grasp. While Hunt knew for pragmatic reasons that the Holston Conference's financial support was crucial for the institution's survival, his convictions regarding the church-relatedness of the college were centered elsewhere. It was simply definitional that church-related meant church-connected with the mutual accountability that such connectedness entailed.

Alongside the curriculum, the church-related college must present "a positive and winsome evangelical" emphasis on the campus. "In a climate devoid of fanatical extremism and capable of reflecting with realism upon the problems of today's society, a sane, reasonable, and authentically spiritual presentation of the claims of Jesus Christ must be offered."[8] It is never the proper role of the church-related institution to enforce response, Hunt on various occasions insisted, but it is the college's responsibility to present a persuasive witness. After all, history bears witness to the fact that many of the reformations of the church, including the Wesleyan revival, have begun on university campuses.

Hunt continued over the years to argue for and defend the church-related college or university as a necessary component of the church's mission. His rationale for the church-related college continued to follow the logic of his inaugural address. The inclusive vision of Christian mission was of necessity focused upon Christ as the origin and goal of mission. If that was true for the inclusive mission, then individual aspects of the general mission should follow the same pattern, and the mission of the church-related college is no exception.

The young college president of 1956, now a bishop in 1970, found himself addressing two significant academic convocations, one in Tennessee at Lambuth and the other in North Carolina at Duke. The fundamental logic of his argument defending church-related higher education as a component of the total mission of the church had been constructed fifteen years earlier. In fact, Hunt had repeated his argument in a carefully reasoned defense of Christian higher education in *The Emory University Quarterly* in 1967. Here Hunt pushed hard for a "real difference" between the church-related university and independent or state-supported institutions. Toward the end of his reflections he pondered, "Is it possible, current trends being what they are, that we may expect to see a virtual end to the merely church-related institution of higher learning during the next few decades, but at the same time the vigorous reappearance of the Christian institution of higher learning?"[9] Hunt was not pressing for a doctrinaire, sectarian higher education. Rather, he was questioning the assumptions of a neutral, "radical freedom" of intellectual inquiry, which in effect made sharp distinctions between the university of reason and the church of faith. The Christian institution of higher education that he envisioned was closer to his original understanding of "the redemptive process" centered in Jesus Christ and extending "to the entire educational experience."

Hunt's 1970 statements in different styles, one an address and the other a sermon, find him playing variations on the same theme he had struck earlier. On April 2 he was at Lambuth College to address the Bishop's Convocation on Christian Higher Education, called by Bishop H. Ellis Finger Jr., resident bishop of the Nashville Area, and the Conference Board of Education, to help the ministers and selected lay leaders of the Memphis Annual Conference and the faculty, students, and trustees of Lambuth College "to consider the pluralistic system of higher education in America; the reason for private, church-related colleges and the aims and purposes of Lambuth College" in the last third of the twentieth century. Hunt's responsibility in the symposium was appropriately to deal with "the reason for private, church-related colleges."[10]

"If the Christian college survives in our time," Hunt declared, "it will do so because of its unashamed involvement with the Christian message and its capacity to bring into the total educational experience a priceless additional ingredient not to be found anywhere else."[11] Lest the rhetoric should sound out of place in the 1970s, Hunt found some hope in campus student unrest, although he was generally a cautious critic of such behavior. One legitimate cause for such unrest may very well be the "grim unwillingness of many American educational institutions to consider sweeping curricular and degree program reforms."[12] Hunt's remarks were a clear indication that while the foundational principle of Christian higher education stood fixed, grounded in the "redemptive process," functions or implementation of the principle was always subject to critical review and revision.

At Lambuth a new note entered Hunt's defense of Christian higher education. To the list of subsidiary arguments, Hunt added the recognition of the importance of the historic duality of the private-public system of higher education, with its invaluable structure of checks and balances. As one component of this duality, historically the church-related college or university had played what may be called the "role of conscience" to public institutions at the points of value articulation and the concept of commitment. It is important, as Hunt expanded his argument, to insist that "church-related higher education may be, in the end, the most trustworthy custodian of academic freedom—which, properly understood and freed from the abuse of irresponsible revolutionaries in academic attire, is a religious principle."[13]

On Sunday, October 18, Bishop Hunt preached in the Duke Chapel where later that day Terry Sanford was to be installed as the new president of the university. Hunt sermonized his argument for church-related higher education by graphically telling the story of Ezekiel who, with a "glimpse of glory" given by God in a vision, sought to reconcile the vision with the nitty-gritty world of the Hebrew exiles in Babylon. "What a picture of today," Hunt exclaimed. "What a picture of higher education endeavoring to apply its vision of knowledge and its meaning to a new day, a new generation, a new earth! . . . Surely one of the critical missions of the Church and the church-related university at this moment is to discover effective ways to bridge that gap." His sermon concluded with an admonition: "And who will say that this undertaking, both in its terrifying complexity and its awful simplicity, is not the major business of church-related universities and their presidents—indeed, the major business of all of us who are here today?"[14]

What Hunt could not foresee on his inauguration day in 1957 were the staggering challenges and pressures that the church-related college would face in the immediate future in maintaining its institutional life. The church-related sector had been the major force in higher education through the period of World War II. Following the war, two major factors arose, challenging some fundamental assumptions of church-related higher education. The postwar GI Bill assisted veterans in obtaining further education that would not have been possible otherwise. Coupled with this development was the rising middle class with educational expectations the extent of which had been unknown before. State-supported institutions of higher education began dramatic expansion. The new phenomenon of state-supported community colleges rapidly developed. For the church-related institutions the first consequence of this expansion of state-supported education was clearly economic. State-supported institutions could provide an education for considerably less in dollars than was the case with the private institutions. Church-related institutions faced competition with public institutions unlike any prior experience in their history.

At the same time the costs of a college education were spiraling. Changes in the tax laws threatened to reduce income from the private philanthropy sector. The private institutions found themselves increasingly dependent upon grants and aid from state and federal monies. Governmental regulations governing such grants threatened the autonomy that the private institutions historically had assumed. Some church-related institutions acquired independent status to relieve the economic pressures and to avoid what seemed to be compromises with their church identity.

The college president did not have the luxury of disassociating himself from these real economic challenges. By the 1970s Hunt, following other United Methodist administrators such as President Paul Hardin III at Wofford College, attempted to balance the federal Constitution's principle of "separation of church and state" with the claim of an implicit constitutional principle of "equal protection under the law." "If the private or church-related college is forced out of business by the public institution because the latter charges a dramatically lower tuition than the former, and if this is made possible by heavy subsidy of the public institution from tax funds," Hunt questioned, "is this principle of equal protection under the law then violated?"[15]

As if economic challenges were not enough, Hunt saw the church-related college confronted with the increasing secularization of the society accompanied with a new kind of anti-intellectualism. The rising secularism could be seen in the decline in the numbers of young people with any background in formation of faith and values that in former days had been the province of the church. For example, the numbers of students in the church-related colleges preparing for church-related vocations decreased. That was not the whole picture by any means. Rising secularism carried with it the values of materialistic acquisition, which translated into increasing numbers of students seeking career skills for "making a living" rather than a liberal arts grounding equipping them for "living a life." The economic pressures and the pressures for recruiting more students tempted the church-related institution to alter its historic educational philosophy. Utilitarian education was Hunt's term for the contemporary alternative, and he was strongly opposed to it. "Purely utilitarian education can teach the human mind how to function technically, mechanically, but," he insisted, "it can never instruct it in the finely tempered skills of rational thought."[16] If the church-related college were to succumb to the temptation of the pragmatic, it would come dangerously close to losing its definitional and functional identity as a Christian college.

To make matters more complicated, the new generation of

students arrived in the college classroom with considerably less mastery of the basic learning skills such as reading, grammar, and mathematics. Hunt knew firsthand the frustrations of faculty when confronted with this problem. He also knew the inherent dangers to a college's allegiance to academic excellence if it capitulated to the times. Above all, a college was not a remedial institution that inflated student grades to maintain its economic viability. These problems were critical for the church, the college, and human civilization itself—"far more critical than the average local church member knows," cautioned Hunt, "and often more serious than the Christian minister has stopped to realize."[17]

Would the church rise to the occasion with renewed energies in support of its mission in higher education? For Hunt, this was the most important question of all. The church's love affair with higher education seemed to be moving into a twilight zone. Some were claiming that while church-related higher education had been a legitimate goal for the church's mission in the nineteenth and early twentieth centuries, that claim could no longer be sustained. The economic pressures were too great, and the horizon of Christian mission had so expanded that other priorities were pushing the educational priority aside. Hunt, however, would not surrender to this argument.

If anything, the mission of the church required the church's engagement in higher education more than ever before. The temptation to bypass liberal education for technical knowledge, to focus higher education more and more upon the practical, the professional, the utilitarian, was to surrender to a technological society where technique, not the person, was the consuming value. The person-centered goals of the liberal arts are "alien accents in today's activistic vernacular."

Hunt, the Christian educator, pleaded:

The strictly personal has vanished in the chorus of the crowds, just as religion's individual pietism has surrendered to the massive involvement neurosis of the moment. But in a world where peoples are initially individuals, and where single votes still determine policy among free persons, who shall say that one day the cacophony of noises from huddled humanity en masse shall not cease, and the regal significance of the person and the person's scale of values be sensed once more? This is the precious, timeless meaning of the liberal arts, the glory of the little college.[18]

The Christian knows, reflected Hunt, that the only satisfying answer to the query regarding the meaning of the human person is in the message of Jesus Christ, and "this equips the Christian college, the church-related college, uniquely to deal effectively wherever the identity crisis presents itself. . . . Our religion teaches us that every person, even the sinner, the mixed-up rebel and the stupid fool, is of infinite worth—one for whom the Son of God died."[19] The unique task of the Christian college is to express that philosophy and policy in actuality.

In the midst of shifting missional agendas, Hunt's voice was being heard repeatedly and almost relentlessly crying for Christian higher education as a priority in contemporary mission. In the transition from the pastorate to a college presidency he learned quickly the intricacies of academia. His reputation as a college administrator rose in the church. What is more significant, however, is that the church found in Hunt one of its most articulate spokespersons for the historic mission of higher education. In a time when church-related colleges sought a softer and more diffused statement of their mission, Hunt hammered away at a more classic definition of the Christian college. In a time when the church-related identity of the college became more vague and evasive, Hunt militantly insisted upon the distinctive "recognizability" of the church-related college.

Hunt was familiar with the major studies of church-related colleges undertaken during the 1960s. He did not get lost in the maze of statistics and conflicting prognostications. Forged through direct experience and critical study, his position of the continuing necessity of the church's engagement in higher education remained unabated.

Hunt's lines of defense for the missional importance of the church-related college were in place long before the appearances of recent historical analyses of the church-related institutions offered by George Marsden in *The Soul of the American University*[20] or James T. Burtchaell in *The Dying of the Light: The Disengagement of Colleges and Universities from Their Christian Churches.*[21] In one sense, he did not need them. He was already convinced that the *raison d'être* of the church-related college had to consist in more than the attempt to make the institutions less sectarian and more inclusive by emphasizing common moral qualities rather than particular Christian theological affirmations. There was a compelling theological argument for Christian higher education as a missional priority for a mainline Protestant church. He had charted his course as early as the inaugural address in 1957. At the heart of the church-related college's mission is the acknowledgment of "the relevance of God and the redemptive process centering in Jesus Christ and His Person and work to the entire educational experience."

His experience as an educator and advocate for Christian higher education brought him recognition in the form of honorary degrees from seven United Methodist institutions (Bethune-Cookman, Drew, Duke, Emory, Emory and Henry, Florida Southern, and Lambuth), one from a Presbyterian school (Tusculum), one from a Roman Catholic institution (Belmont Abbey), and one from the University of Chattanooga (once a Methodist school and now a division of the University of Tennessee).

Hunt's stature as an educator was highly regarded within the Council of Bishops and the College of Bishops of the Southeastern Jurisdiction. For this reason he was selected by the Southeastern College of Bishops to represent them on the Search Committee for a new dean of Candler School of Theology in 1968. Hunt was a logical choice to represent the College of Bishops. He was a graduate of Candler, he served on the board of trustees of the university, and he possessed the academic experience.

With the election of William Cannon to the episcopacy, the position of dean of Candler School of Theology was vacated effective on August 31. In the interim Dr. Mack B. Stokes served as acting dean. President Sanford Atwood concurred with the College of Bishops' choice of Hunt. The Search Committee was instructed to submit several names, and from this list the president would recommend one person to the board of trustees of the university.

The process was long and necessarily thorough. More than fifty names of prospects surfaced. During the process of narrowing the slate of possibilities to the president's desired number, Atwood told Hunt that he did not intend to continue Candler's tradition of calling deans from within the faculty. Bishop Ellis Finger of the Nashville Area and Hunt's longtime friend from Holston, Ben St. Clair, who was then senior pastor of West End Church in Nashville, drew Hunt's attention to Dr. James T. Laney, an assistant professor of Christian ethics and director of Methodist studies in the Divinity School of Vanderbilt University. Hunt shared Laney's name with the

Search Committee. Laney's name had been on a long list but had not received serious consideration because he was an unknown in the Southeast. After interviews with the Search Committee, Laney was placed on the short list that the president received. In the spring of 1969 Atwood, with the approval of the university's board of trustees, announced the appointment of Laney as the new dean.

Some members of the College of Bishops were disappointed that Stokes had not been selected. In fact, along with his episcopal colleagues, Hunt had favored the selection of Stokes and so represented the thinking of the College of Bishops to the Search Committee in its early sessions. Hunt was able to interpret the selection process to the college and to assure them that Stokes's record as a veteran member of the faculty, thirteen years as associate dean, and for some months as acting dean was esteemed by faculty and administration alike. The president's decision to select a new dean from outside the faculty had been a matter of principle. Furthermore, Laney had been chosen solely on the basis of merit and was elected because of who he was and what he was. Hunt maintained his close friendship with Stokes, and from the time of Laney's installation he and Hunt developed a relationship of mutual respect and friendship, culminating in the efforts of Laney and Dean Waites to bring Hunt as a Bishop in Residence and Visiting Professor to Candler's campus upon his retirement.

Within the Council of Bishops, Hunt was called upon repeatedly to give guidance and leadership in matters pertaining to higher education and theological education. The fact that the council appointed Hunt to convene and anticipated his subsequent election as the chair of the 1984–1988 General Conference Committee on Our Theological Task is indicative of their respect for his academic and theological merits. Hunt was

requested to compose for the council's adoption its 1998 statement, "The United Methodist Church and Its Relationship to Its
Academic Institutions."

From 1980 to 1984 Hunt served as president of the General
Board of Higher Education and Ministry. A close team relationship between him and Dr. F. Thomas Trotter, general secretary
of the board, quickly developed. Together they worked toward
providing church-based legal consultation services for colleges
and universities, and called the church toward the goal of a $100
million scholarship fund for United Methodist college students.

To those who know Earl Hunt from afar, he appears an enig-
ma—a bafflement and a puzzle. He can at one moment be an
eloquent advocate of evangelism and in the next moment mount
an impressive argument for the "glory of the lighted mind." The
bafflement may be more a commentary on conditions within the
church than a polar tension within Hunt's mind. In the church
evangelism and its proponents have too often exhibited an anti-
intellectualism, driving a wedge between heart and mind. On
the other hand, academicians have distanced themselves from
evangelism, regarding evangelism as intellectually suspect.

The fact that Hunt should join the two as he did across his
ministry in the parish, on the college campus, and in the episcopacy should be no great mystery. He stood in a tradition stretch-
ing from the early Greek Fathers who could pen a carefully
reasoned defense of the faith while preaching passionate sermons, to Martin Luther writing his biblical commentaries while
preaching the watchword of the Reformation—"justification by
grace through faith"—to John Wesley, an Oxford don transformed into the leading voice of the evangelical revival, to
Charles Finney, the most important evangelist of the American
church in the nineteenth century who eventually became the
president of Oberlin College.

The religious environment in which Hunt's mind and character were shaped did not know this bifurcation between religious conversion and intellectual nurture. Those early Methodists in the East Tennessee valleys could experience an impassioned sermon and altar call on Sunday and found a college on Monday without the slightest sense of incongruity in their actions. Whether they were consciously aware of the Wesleyan synthesis of heart and mind, they were intuitively Wesleyan in their understanding of created human nature with heart and mind conjoined, sinful human nature diseased in heart and mind, and redeemed human nature restored by divine love to a right heart and mind. In his practice of ministry Hunt had never sensed a tension, much less a gap, between his study lined with his beloved biographies and the pulpit from which he preached the saving grace of Christ.

On a profounder level, for Hunt, the unity of the two, evangelism and education, heart and mind, had to do with the Christ to whom one was committed. In other words, the unity of which Hunt spoke was found in his Christology, his belief in the person and work of Christ. Wesley in his day had admonished his preachers to preach "the fullness of Christ"—Christ in all his offices as Prophet, Priest, and King. Without employing the Wesleyan categories, Hunt sought in his preaching to proclaim "the fullness of Christ" in Incarnation, Cross, and Resurrection.

The record of the church has not been exemplary in holding to such christological fullness. Nineteenth-century revivalism called sinners to repentance under a picture of Jesus as the crucified substitutionary sacrifice minus the Jesus of the Sermon on the Mount and the call of the resurrected Christ to a life of discipleship. A fuller picture would have made plain that one cannot have Jesus as Savior unless one simultaneously embraces him as Lord. The liberal theological tradition, which has been a

dominant theological influence in the shaping of higher education, pictured a Jesus who was the prophet of the moral law and
the supreme teacher of ethical values. In this picture the reverse
of the former was the case; liberals sought a Lord whose inspiration would be the means of their salvation. With different
Jesuses, no wonder that evangelism and education should come
to be separate and different spheres of the church's life!

Hunt found his christological picture in the Gospel narratives
running from Incarnation through the earthly ministry of the
proclamation and enactment of the Kingdom to the Cross, and
from the Cross to Resurrection and Pentecost. The power of the
biblical narrative was greater than any one doctrinal formulation. The story of a Bethlehem night, a Galilean ministry, a
Calvary crucifixion, and a garden Resurrection conveyed "Christ
in his fullness." It was this picture from which Hunt could not
escape. Even in his seminary days, he was able to integrate the
historical-critical method of liberals with an evangelical understanding of the person and work of Christ. To Hunt, it was
inconceivable that the church should practice an evangelism of
a Calvary without a Galilee or support an educational ministry of
a Galilee without a Calvary. In his mind evangelism without education is dangerous, and education without evangelism is sterile.
In reality, Hunt, the evangelist, and Hunt, the educator, are not
two personalities but one integral mind in which, in Lynn
Harold Hough's words, "evangelicalism is intelligence on fire."

Chapter Nine

Believer

I am not first of all a bishop, or even a minister; I am a sinner saved by grace," reflected Earl Hunt on the eve of his seventy-eighth birthday.[1] The seventy-eight years had been a pilgrimage of faith marked by a keen personal awareness of divine leading and prompting, a pilgrimage in which many of God's servants had "tapped his shoulder" on the way.

A story of contrasts, attributed to the late Swiss theologian Karl Barth, assists in understanding Earl Hunt's personal formation of faith. The story describes two men watching the fitful gyrations of a bee reputed to possess a deadly sting. One man observes the bee's antics with a calm and assured composure, while the other man exhibits a dreadful fear lest he be stung. The difference between the two observers is that one knows that the bee has already stung and, hence, has lost its deadly venom to inflict further harm; the other has no knowledge of this fact and can only experience dread lest the bee sting again.

Whatever may be the origin of the story, it illustrates two fundamental ways in which human beings come to faith. Some persons, struggling with an overwhelming sense of guilt, fear, or meaninglessness, come to faith through a dramatic and powerful experience of conversion eventuating in radical changes in their self-understanding and lifestyle. For others the experience of conversion comes gradually and more gently as a persuasive

Presence brings a new perspective on who they are as creatures of God's grace. Both ways of coming to faith are equally valid. The versatile grace of God meets persons where they are and pervades their lives in ways appropriate to who they are.

Hunt's faith story differs in significant ways from the faith story of a Luther or a Wesley. A Luther agonizingly struggles to find a gracious God until one day in a Wittenberg study cubicle he fastens upon the words of Saint Paul, "The just shall live by faith," and the words ring with personal certitude. A Wesley searches for a sense of faith assurance until he comes to Aldersgate Street, and a year later he begins an itinerant ministry in which the poor hear him gladly and bear witness to the amazing grace of Christ in their lives. Gradually, Wesley's anxiety about faith assurance recedes as others through their experience of assurance become a means of grace to him. Other persons, including Hunt, witness to less traumatic struggles. Having been baptized and nurtured in a faith community, these persons gradually find themselves "found by God" and affirm their "blessed assurance." That was the experience of Hunt.

As a teenager, alone in his parents' home in Johnson City on a Sunday afternoon, Hunt knelt by his parents' bed and asked God to forgive his sin and take his life into God's care. He had been baptized as an infant, and at the age of twelve he had received confirmation instruction and had joined the church. Prior to that Sunday afternoon, he had been engaged in thought and prayer for days and weeks. "Quite suddenly," he says, "it all seemed to come together for me." It was no casual matter, nor was the moment punctuated with dramatic evidences of God's power. It was a calm and deliberate act on his part. It was nonetheless a discernible "shining moment" that he never forgot. "I arose satisfied, calm, and resolute in the action I had taken."[2]

Hunt's "coming to faith" had more the character of continuity than discontinuity. His pilgrimage was marked more by gradual development, each experience contributing cumulatively to the next, than by distinctive episodes. To be sure, during his early college years, he experienced a period of doubt and skepticism, which seems to have been more intellectual than experiential. It was not what many call "the dark night of the soul." Even during this period of doubt, he continued to involve himself in the life of the church, and one of the major factors contributing to the resolution of this doubt was the occasional teaching of his Sunday school class by his professor of science from nearby East Tennessee State. "So it was," says Hunt, "that I returned after a year or two from my post-adolescent odyssey into doubt with a firm and never-since-shaken conviction that God is, indeed, a reality, and that he is a rewarder of all those that diligently seek him (Hebrews 11:6)."[3]

Hunt's call to the ministry was similar to his earlier experience. He preached his first sermon in his home church when he was fourteen years old. Through his teenage years, he weighed the possibilities of six or more vocational decisions. At one time he wanted to become a doctor, but found he did not take well to the study of chemistry. Then he considered the possibilities of careers in architecture, journalism, and forestry. His sense of call to the ministry of the church came in a gradual and progressive manner. "As I think of the calls that have come to other ministers who are my friends," Hunt states, "I must recognize that God's voice summons us in vastly different ways. To some it comes suddenly, sharply, and with unmistakable certainty, often taking the form of a specific experience or event. It did not come to me that way."[4]

In the years following the Sunday afternoon experience of accepting Jesus Christ, Hunt continued a faithful involvement in the life of his church influenced by family and friends. In particular he was fascinated by great preachers and their preaching, which he encountered in the bold project of the Johnson City youth inviting well-known preachers from across the country to preach monthly in citywide interdenominational youth rallies. "Gradually," he says, "I became aware that I must preach, and one day (I cannot put my finger on when it was) I was conscious that my entire being was literally saturated with a sense of God's call."[5]

Hunt's story of faith is characterized and dominated by belief rather than questions and doubt. To be sure, he wrestled with the intellectual questions of faith but always within the environment of a Christian community confessing its faith. From time to time he "traveled the trails of honest doubt, alluring temptation, personal sorrow, and faith's eclipse," but such experiences seem to have been only episodic moments in a continuing journey of faith. His journey was more that of a faithful believer searching for understanding than an anxious doubter seeking faith.

In his seminary years in a liberal-evangelical school he did not experience a wavering of faith when confronted with critical methods of examining the faith that his church had inculcated in him. Historical-critical methods in the study of Scripture did not lessen his conviction that Scripture was nevertheless authoritative for faith and life. He never espoused a literalistic, fundamentalist interpretation of Scripture. He assimilated the critical method within his overarching conviction that Scripture was inspired by God through the medium of fallible human beings.

In later years when his fondness for biography became particularly focused on the great preachers of the faith, his preferences were for the Scottish divines such as Arthur John Gossip, Peter Taylor Forsyth, and James S. Stewart with their strong drive to assert the truths of faith, rather than for the English empiricistic mind frequently fixated with questions and doubts. His favorite American pulpiteers were persons such as David H.

C. Read, George A. Buttrick, and Peter Marshall, the transplanted Scotsman. He had little regard for the theology or preaching of Paul Tillich. The Europeans whom he admired were of the "stripe" of Emil Brunner, Karl Barth, and Helmut Thielicke, rather than the existentialist Rudolf Bultmann and his disciples. His predilections were pointedly expressed in the words of the British Baptist T. R. Glover, frequently quoted by Hunt, "I won't give tuppence for the man who goes into the pulpit to tell me what my duty is, but I'll give all for the man who goes into the pulpit to tell me whence my help comes!"[6]

Although continuity and development are characteristics of Hunt's faith journey, he felt some stresses and tensions. These dynamics appear not so much in the formation of Hunt's faith convictions as in his strong efforts to apply his faith in mission. Others could and did speak of faith as rising from the caldron of doubt. Hunt did not question the fact that this is the experience of many persons, and he took care to be sensitive to the doubts of sincere, searching persons. But he countered the skepticism and agnosticism that he found in the contemporary secularized society with a quick criticism and dismissal: "God absent from his creation? What an illusion—what a lie! Only those, it seems to me, who have allowed their minds to be blinded to life itself could possibly overlook the many evidences to the contrary."[7] He believed that he had more important tasks than to dwell upon the contemporary "temporal"; he had an urgent message from the transcendent "eternal."

The tension in Hunt's faith was not with doubt but involved his Wesleyan drive to forge a "faith active in love." His struggles focused on his great concern to assure that the faith proclaimed was also the faith embodied in ministry to and for the world. He was "one in spirit" with persons who, on the surface, appeared to espouse theological stances disparate from his own but who fought valiantly to apply their faith in missional engagement in the contemporary world. From as early as his seminary period he embraced the evangelistic passion of a Dwight L. Moody, who insisted that God had placed him in a tiny boat upon tempestuous seas with the command, "Dwight, rescue as many people as you can." And in the Council of Bishops he shepherded the project of the writing of the biography of Bromley Oxnam, whose liberal theology was certainly not of Hunt's disposition but whose passion for the reform of the social order was at one with Hunt's missional conscience.

Hunt's persistent arguing of a case for Christian higher education brought him into constant contact with persons whose theological perspectives were quite different from his own but whose commitment to the mission of higher education was close to his heart. His struggle with effecting a missional incarnation of his evangelical faith placed him repeatedly in the midst of the polarities that threatened the church's life. He did not for political or pragmatic reasons intentionally place himself in these situations. Something drove him there. Whether the missional fronts were evangelism, social reform, or higher education, the struggle between belief and action, between faith and mission, inescapably cast him into the role of the bridger of the gaps.

Hunt's faith convictions were tried and tested in the crucible of everyday experience. These faith convictions did not so much arise from experience, but rather his faith convictions illuminated experience revealing experience's deeper dimensions. In spite of his formal theological education in a moderately liberal seminary, he really did not agree with the liberal theological enterprise that from the days of Friedrich Schleiermacher, the progenitor of Protestant liberal theology, had sought to derive doctrine from experience. Hunt's method—if he had one and he denied that he did—insisted that while doctrinal belief interpreted experience and was confirmed by experience, experience did not produce the precious doctrines of his faith. His personal orthodox convictions were basically "once delivered," and for the most part were the Wesleyan themes he had heard in the church of his upbringing. That they were inextricably enmeshed with experience he had no doubts; that they were in effect produced from experience did not accord with his understanding of the church's message. From experience he could mount an argument to defend a doctrine, but right doctrine was always initially derived from the self-revelation of God in Jesus Christ. Here he was more with Karl Barth than with Protestant liberals. Or perhaps his seminary professor Franklin Nutting Parker's descriptive way of unfolding the doctrines of the faith had been the dominant influence.

Hunt was concluding his four-year term as resident bishop of the Nashville Area when in 1980 he put in writing the principal beliefs that had guided his ministry. The result was a book entitled *I Have Believed: A Bishop Talks About His Faith,*[8] the scope of which he confessed could be summarized in the words of Norman Macleod of the Barony of Glasgow, "There is a Father in heaven who loves us, a Brother Savior who died for us, a Spirit who helps us to be good, and a Home where we shall all meet at last."[9]

Hunt repeatedly raised the disclaimer that he was a tutored theologian, and yet when he put himself to the task of offering a personal theological statement, he arranged the topics and chapters according to the traditional order of systematic theology beginning with God and proceeding to Jesus Christ, the Holy Spirit, prayer, faith, the kingdom of God, and eternal life.

In reality his personal faith developed and unfolded in a somewhat different manner. From his earliest days his faith rested upon the certainties of a loving God revealed in a saving Son confirmed by the witness of the Holy Spirit. Continuity with this early faith-formation is confirmed by his statement in later years, "For better or for worse, the basic structure of my original belief, although no longer wholly untutored, has not been altered materially. Perhaps one never gets entirely away from those first vivid exposures to religious reality."[10]

Hunt's faith was firmly anchored in his belief in Jesus Christ. "A great portion of my Christian creed," he acknowledges, "has always rested upon a foundation of humble certainty about my Saviour."[11] His first thoughts about Jesus were that of a Friend, and even as he matured and confessed that Jesus Christ was his Savior, the latter idea had room in it for Leslie Weatherhead's notion of "transforming friendship."

The bishop's personal faith in Jesus Christ oscillates between the two poles of the power of Jesus Christ in human life and the biblical witness to the incarnate Son of God, crucified and risen. Hunt points to Wesley's own preaching: "If someone had asked him [Wesley] to prove the divinity of Christ, he would probably have pointed to some humble convert, to some little band of men and women whose sins were forgiven and in whose faces shone the light which was reflected from the face of Christ."[12] Yet Christianity begins with the biggest idea the human mind has ever been asked to enfold: "No one has ever seen God; but God's only Son, he who is nearest to the Father's heart, he has made him known" (John 1:18 NEB).

Seeing Jesus Christ, we see the Father: "Anyone who has seen me has seen the Father" (John 14:9 NEB). The incarnate Christ is forever the Divine Indicative that God in Jesus in meeting human beings on the human level has stooped down to the deepest depths of their need.

That God has so stooped to the deepest depths of human need is seen in the crucifixion of Christ. Quoting one of his favorite British Reformed theological guides, John S. Whale,

Hunt writes: "He who died there was Incarnate Righteousness and Love; no less."[13] On Calvary God gathered together all human history in a tiny period of time. "This," the bishop confidently claims, "is really why the stupendous meaning of the cross is far too staggering for our little minds to grasp. And this is the reason it is big enough to save us."[14]

Calvary as the unique saving event is confirmed by God's act of Resurrection. The Resurrection validates the "gospel's cause" and strengthens "those who labor in it." Drawing again from his gallery of Scottish divines, Hunt quotes James S. Stewart, "There had now appeared, in the midst of time, life in a new dimension. . . . The heralds of the Resurrection were not merely preaching it as fact: they were living in it as in a new country."[15]

So foundational for Hunt's personal faith is his belief in a "Brother Savior who has died for us" that the traditional theological arguments for the existence of God to which he subscribes, such as the adaptive interaction of nature, the nature of being, the intelligence of design and the presence of the moral law, pale in the light of the revelation of God in Jesus Christ. These arguments seem to have helped in relieving his brief postadolescent period of doubt, but even then he was sustained by his continued participation in the life of the church. In truth, these theistic arguments have their full credibility when in the revelation of Jesus Christ one beholds "the Father in heaven who loves us." "I know," affirms the bishop, "God exists."

> I know because, in spite of its sinfulness, the human spirit can be hospitable to concepts of beauty, truth, goodness, and compassion— ideas nearer to heaven than to earth.
>
> I know because I have seen so many wasted lives redeemed and remade.
>
> But I believe in God most of all because I see him in the face of Jesus Christ.

I have never believed in Jesus because of the miracles. I can believe in the miracles because of Jesus. He is the greatest miracle, and I simply cannot account for him apart from the fact that God has to be real.[16]

To believe in Jesus Christ and not affirm belief in the Holy Spirit, Hunt knows, is to court an abstraction. The Holy Spirit's work is to make real and convincing in the present the saving grace of the crucified and risen Savior.

[From] the moment I accept Jesus Christ and am pardoned by God, thus receiving assurance of my salvation, my life becomes a place of residence for the Spirit of God. He begins his work of grace within me, helping me to face up to my own temptations and shortcomings and enabling me, through a power quite beyond myself, to grow and develop into the kind of Christian I ought to be.[17]

Hunt knows from past and present experience that the belief in the Holy Spirit has occasioned dissensions and divisions in the life of the church. He knows about the holiness controversies regarding perfection or entire sanctification in nineteenth-century American Methodism. He also knows firsthand of disruptions caused by some "baptized in the Spirit" charismatics in the present. His irenic spirit enables him to distinguish between the overenthusiastic espousals of the Holy Spirit's work and genuine workings of the Spirit bringing persons to purity of motive and the gifts of the Spirit. He affirms the latter by claiming as valid what builds up the Body of Christ. He does not doubt the experience; he turns his critical eye to the uses to which the experience is put. He, therefore, does not set himself over or against holiness and Pentecostal doctrine. While professing neither perfection nor speaking in tongues, he nonetheless affirms the best of these traditions as the Spirit's rich contribution to the corporate faith of the people of God. Furthermore, he knows the all-too-often spiritless congregation and its parched ground. He longs for a renewal of the Spirit in the life of the congregation, but he recognizes that this will not come without a price: "If people like you and me are to join effectively in this effort and quest, it will require of us a radical and revolutionary deepening of Christian commitment. There is a high price to be paid, as all the real saints who have ever walked the glory road with God have discovered. My question to my own soul is whether or not I am willing to pay such a price."[18]

The creed says, "I believe in the resurrection." That for Hunt is sufficient. While there are philosophical and psychological arguments for life beyond death, these are interesting but not sufficient. Because the Christian believes in Jesus Christ, the Christian believes in the resurrection of Jesus Christ as the ground of human hope in eternal life. "Therefore, for myself and all other Christians," says Hunt, "the final assurance of the reality of eternal life comes not from any arguments of reason or scientific documentation, but rather from a deliberate and intentional act of faith in the fact of the resurrection of Jesus Christ."[19] We have no blueprint of heaven, but we do have "appetizing hints," to use Arthur John Gossip's phrase. To be claimed by the revelation and power of the grace of Jesus Christ and the witness to his resurrection is sufficient ground for our hope for future life.

Hopeful faith in eternal life is not contrary to, but exceeds, the limits of conscious reason. Such faith springs from a deeper realm where the heart has reasons the mind knows not. Human finitude poses a perplexing question for young and old alike. The attempt to speak the word of Christian hope is a demanding one. To stretch human words to speak of eternal realities seems to bring the human words to a breaking point. Words are time-bound, and eternity is beyond the boundary. How then shall faith speak? As with creation language, so with the witness to eternal life, the believer utilizes the metaphorical language of faith, pictures, and analogies to speak of the beyond. That such can be done in simple and childlike (not childish) ways Hunt demonstrated in the early days of his ministry. In a pastoral letter to a little girl, whose grandmother, the wife of a former mayor of Atlanta, had died, he wrote his credo on eternal life:

Dear Margaret:

I must tell you something which may be a bit hard for you to understand, something which will seem at first very sad. But if you learn to look at it as I hope you will, then you will see that really it is quite beautiful and wonderful.

Let me begin by telling you about our two homes. One of them is here on earth, the one that we now have—where Father and Mother are. It is the one our bodies use. We can see it and sense it. The other Home is far more wonderful than this one. It is the Home of our souls. We cannot see it just yet, but we can sometimes sense it. Our heavenly Father is there. Jesus is there, too. And many of our friends are there. It is a very beautiful and a very wonderful place where there is no trouble, no sadness, no wrong, no pain. Can you remember how the sunrise looks on a lovely morning? Try to imagine a home as perfect and as bright as the sunrise. The Home of our souls is more than that. It is all the beauty, gladness, peace, and joy that God can bring together in one place. It's so wonderful that we call it heaven.

There comes a time when we are through with our homes here—the homes our bodies use—and are ready to go on to the Home of our souls. If we have trusted in Jesus, it is a beautiful journey with our hand in God's hand all the way, and nothing can happen to us as we travel. When we get to this better Home, our real joy and happiness begin. Everything unpleasant is forgotten, and a whole new life opens before us. Our old friends are there-some of them will meet us and others will be coming all the while. And best of all, God himself is there to take care of us forever. Forever is a long word, isn't it? But that's what I mean. The Home of our souls is so wonderful that we will never want to leave it, and the best part of it is we won't have to leave it—it belongs to us forever.

You've been wondering about your Grandmother. She isn't here, and you haven't quite understood where she is. You remember how sick she was, don't you? Well, that was when God saw it was better for her to go to her other Home, and now she is there with him. She lived such a good and rich life here in her home on earth that she was ready for her other Home long before the rest of us. Her heavenly Father took her in his arms and carried her away to the Home he had ready for her. When his Son was here many years ago, he told us about it: "In my Father's house are many mansions," he said, "if it were not so, I would have told you. I go to prepare a place for you, and if I go to prepare a place for you, I will come again and receive you unto myself. . . ." And that's where Grandmother is. We know she is happy, for she always loved to be with God in his house, the church, and when she read his word and prayed. And we know she isn't sick anymore, for people don't get sick in this other Home—ever. And we know she is waiting for us.

One of these days, likely a good many years from now, we shall be ready to go to her. We won't die, although you will hear people who don't know any better use that word. Grandmother didn't die—never let anybody tell you that she did. Nobody who loves Jesus and trusts him ever really dies—nobody. She simply went with God to her other Home—her soul's Home. And that's what we shall do when God decides that we have finished with our homes here. And then we shall be with her always. Until that time, we must remember that Grandmother is really "God's Guest" in a place lovelier than any we have ever visited. It will be lonely without her, but we can bear that loneliness when we know where she is and know, too, that one day, if we share her faith in God and Jesus, we shall be there.

Very sincerely your friend,
Your Grandmother's Pastor[20]

Some would call this eschatological faith. Quite simply it is the faith of one who is confident of God's faithfulness in the past, who experiences that divine faithfulness now, and who trusts the same faithfulness of God for the future. For Hunt this is no "pie-in-the-sky-by-and-by" projection whereby one is relieved of any responsibilities, personal or social, in the here and now. Confidence in God's future sets the Christian radically free to act responsibly in the present. "Because we are ready to die, we find that we are suddenly equipped to live as we have never lived before, and for causes—dangerous causes—that are infinitely bigger than we are."[21]

A reader of Hunt's credo may wonder why he did not devote a chapter to the church to which he had committed so much of his time, mind, and energy over the years. Hunt has his reasons for suspending any consideration of the church until he comes to the "epilogue" of his faith-recital. His decision is deliberate. First come the "ultimates" of belief—God, Christ, the Holy Spirit, the experience of forgiveness, the new life in the Spirit, and the hope in life everlasting.

The conclusion should not be drawn that the church is an appendage to a recital of belief. Rather, it is the medium through belief has been made possible. The church is the witness, the pointer to belief, and it is the community within which belief again and again becomes lived faith. Because it is "penultimate" rather than "ultimate," the church is of crucial importance for belief. The church is of God in the form of the "earthen vessel" so that if faith boasts, faith will not boast of itself or the church, but faith will boast of its Lord.

The church is the divinely chosen means toward God's ultimate future. Hunt makes this clear: "I do not mean for a moment to deprecate organized religion or the church as an institution. I understand that every great dynamic concept which functions in human society must have its institutional housing. Education needs the school, health-care the hospital, love between a man and a woman the home—and religion its 'tent of testimony' (Numbers 9:15) or church."[22] In this sense church is never an article of faith in the same way as God, Christ, and the Spirit are.

Whatever the size and character of the congregation, whatever the polity of the denomination, whatever the structures of its organization—these are relative. The church is always "between the times" of Christ's first and final appearing. In this sense it is always the means to the end. "I believe with all my heart the structure of the church should be subordinated constantly to its mission."[23] With this bottom-line statement Hunt returns to the perennial struggle of his personal faith. He is confident in the faithfulness of God, assured of his acceptance by Christ, and constantly growing in the Spirit. Hunt's struggle is with faith seeking to "missionize" itself. In truth Hunt's struggle has always been with the church—the church that had birthed and nurtured him in faith and that at the same time resisted, kicking and screaming, God's command to witness to and for the world. He constantly tugged and pulled the church to become what Wesley had envisioned, "faith active in love."

His has been a persistent struggle to awaken a slumbering church to its duty and responsibility to communicate the good news with effectiveness and with urgency to individuals and society. "I believe that human nature can be changed, and the tormenting problems of the world addressed and solved."[24] That is his confident belief in the working of divine grace when the church willingly becomes the instrument of that grace.

Hunt, a bishop of the church, is troubled: "My part of the church, perhaps as a result of unintentional insensitivity, has seemed recently to phrase its theology, design its program, and in general conduct its ministry more for the benefit of the few than for the many."[25] The church, his United Methodist Church, has at times, particularly in the present moment, lost both its evangelistic nerve and its voice to proclaim the grace of Christ to those outside. Too often it has thought its evangelistic mission to be completed with confirmations and transfers of church membership. At times the church has sought the security of "civil" religion, relinquishing its responsibility to address prophetically the social order regnant with racism, sexism, and poverty, when in God's economy it is commanded to speak and act with its best understanding of biblical and Christian insights.

Exactly here is the locus of Hunt's struggle of faith. Whatever the form of the church's mission, and he has clearly staked the fronts of evangelism, social engagement, and higher education, the missional passion springs from a saving awareness of God in Jesus Christ. "Not to recognize this is to invite missional disaster," Hunt warned the delegates in the opening sermon of the 1988 General Conference. "Great enterprises for God grow in the rich soil of vital belief, intentional spiritual discipline, and steadily renewed exposure to the whole treasury of Christian doctrine."[26]

The church that he loved and served was and would remain the cause of his anguished struggle. Like Jacob wrestling with the mysterious stranger by the Jabbok, Hunt would not let go until the dawning of a new day:

> If I understand my soul correctly, I deeply desire to spend the remainder of my days and all my strength helping the church to become what it ought to be in our time. It has baffling problems and terrifying dilemmas. It is limping like a crippled giant when it ought to be marching like a conquering army. But the darkness of its night is penetrated by the light that was never on land or sea. The church is custodian of the message which is, indeed, the last best hope of earth.[27]

As he neared the celebration of his seventy-eighth birthday Hunt reminisced and concluded, "I must affirm the fact that my Christian faith is stronger now than it has ever been in my life. My creed is still quite simple:

I believe in an all-powerful, all-knowing personal God who has loved us with an everlasting love.

I believe in a person's responsibility before God for his or her thoughts, words, and deeds.

I believe in the salvation of the Cross and in the fact that a human being may know that sin has been forgiven.

I believe in the beauty, purity, and power of the Christian life and in the availability of divine strength for the living of it.

I believe that the purposes of God have meaning in history and will eventually triumph.

I believe in a life beyond this life for the children of God, in which human identity and personality will come to glorious fulfillment."[28]

The words of the prophet Zechariah (9:12) capture the essence of Hunt's faith odyssey. He has always been a "prisoner of hope." Quite simply, he says, "This is my faith."

Epilogue

❧

O n a July morning in 1988 the Southeastern Jurisdiction of The United Methodist Church paid tribute to the bishops retiring from active episcopacy and celebrated their years of service to the church. On the stage that morning were five bishops representing a total of sixty years of episcopal service: Robert M. Blackburn (sixteen years), Paul A. Duffey and Roy C. Clark (eight years each), R. Kern Eustler (four years) and Earl G. Hunt, Jr. (twenty-four years). Rarely does a bishop's tenure span the length of Hunt's. The record of his episcopacy was as full as the years of his tenure. He had witnessed the formation of a new united church. He had led the Southeastern Jurisdiction in the uniting of its annual conferences with the annual conferences of the Central Jurisdiction, thus bringing to an end the system of structural racial segregation. In the meantime he had appointed the first African American district superintendent in the Southeast. For twelve years he had been the United Methodist spokesperson defending the church's ecumenical endeavors of the National Council of Churches. He had watched with pride while six pastors who had served with him in three episcopal areas were elected to the episcopacy: Roy C. Clark in 1980, Ernest A. Fitzgerald, J. Lloyd Knox, and Ernest W. Newman in 1984, and Thomas B. Stockton and Robert H. Spain in 1988. In his retirement he would observe the election of five more of his former pastors: Robert

E. Fannin and William W. Morris in 1992, and Joseph E. Pennel Jr., Charlene P. Kammerer, and J. Lawrence McCleskey in 1996. Six of them—Knox, Newman, Spain, Fannin, Morris, and Kammerer—had been members of Hunt's cabinet in Tennessee or Florida. He had been called upon to be president of both the Southeastern College of Bishops and the Council of Bishops. He had chaired one of the most important General Conference commissions since the merger of 1968—the General Committee on Our Theological Task. Now he was retiring, or so he thought. Speaking for himself and Mary Ann, he concluded his remarks before the jurisdictional conference, "Our life has been a joy and a glory all the way, and we are grateful."

The call to assume the executive leadership of the Foundation for Evangelism in 1989 entailed a schedule as full as that of a presiding bishop. He itinerated across the connectional church, cultivating support for the foundation while extending its programmatic outreach. In this sense, retirement meant that he assumed the role of what could be called an "itinerating bishop." Until recent times, when health would no longer permit, he continued a heavy schedule of preaching engagements in churches large and small.

For understandable reasons, memories of his ministry will conjure many different images. *Hunt was a pastor-preacher.* His vocation from the beginning to the present has been to pastoral ministry. He always saw himself as endeavoring to fulfill that calling. For many the image of his pastoral ministry will always be focused upon his eloquent preaching. Many will continue to remember his sermon preached on many occasions, "Pilate's Washbowl." Yet even while in the episcopacy, he continued to be a pastor to pastors and to many of his colleagues in the Council of Bishops. Nevertheless, the enduring impression has been that of preacher. With meticulous attention to rhetoric, he was a careful wordsmith. His staccato delivery punctuated the power of his conviction. His uncanny sense of timing kept his congregations alert and listening. His former bishop and longtime friend, Roy Short, captured the image of his ministry by saying, "The pulpit is his throne."[1]

Hunt was a careful, cautious administrator. By nature he did not relish making tough decisions, but when times demanded them, he did not allow grass to grow under his feet. He was particularly forceful on issues of race. From the time of his college presidency, he had learned the importance of consultation. He sought to hear the lay voice by creating the Lay Advisory Councils. He listened to his pastors, for example, in the Bishop's Dialogue Sessions, an important component of the Institute for Homiletical Studies in Western North Carolina. He had a "nose" for imminent "crises," sometimes real and at other times imagined. But when real crises lurked, he disarmed them with preparation for resolution.

Hunt was an apostle. Biblically, apostolicity means being sent forth as a messenger or an ambassador. According to Saint Paul, God "apostles" Jesus, and subsequently, God "apostles" the Spirit to the end that the church be "apostled" or sent out as messenger or ambassador.

> But when the time had fully come, God sent forth [apostellein] his Son, born of woman, born under the law, to redeem those who were under the law, so that we might receive adoption as sons. And because you are sons, God has sent [apostellein] the Spirit of his Son into our hearts. (Gal. 4:4-6*a* RSV)

Hunt was not only a student of and strategist for evangelism; he was and continues to be an evangel-apostle in his own person. Bishop Cannon's observations are correct: "Evangelism has been his love . . . since his ordination. This was the heartbeat of his pastoral ministry."[2] Hunt stands in the company of those indomitable Methodist evangelistic laymen, John R. Mott and Harry Denman, and the evangelist-missionary, E. Stanley Jones. He knows his Wesleyan tradition and owns it as his own. As a careful crafter of words, he would probably phrase Francis Asbury's words of 1815 differently, but he would nonetheless wholeheartedly agree: "We will not give up the cause—we will not abandon the world to infidels."[3]

Hunt was a scholar. He never wrote scholarly treatises, and he always protested the appellation of scholar. He was, however, a careful student of history *via* the biographies of history's "greats." He gathered a major collection of biographies of figures secular and religious. These volumes did not collect dust on his study shelves. He read them with an eye of historical discernment. Of worldly possessions he coveted his biographies, along with his autograph collection, above almost anything else. What many persons do not know is that he was a student of Latin and continued to read Latin throughout his busy life. Again, Bishop Cannon's words are apt: "Bishop Hunt has one of the best furnished minds in the church."[4]

Hunt was a church theologian. He was his own particular kind of theologian. The late Albert Outler characterized John Wesley as a "folk theologian." Hunt was an "intuitive theologian." He was not always patient with the theological nuances of the academic theologians, though he professed that Karl Barth, one of the most nuanced theologians of modern times, had exerted major influences on his thinking. His theological syllabus included most of the modern theologians, evangelical, neoorthodox, and liberal. At times he may not have plumbed the depths of their thought, but he certainly ranged the breadth of the theological spectrum.

Hunt was a bishop. Historically, southern Methodist bishops have tended to have a more traditional hierarchical view of episcopacy. Perhaps it was due to his roots in the former Methodist Episcopal Church, but regardless of the ecclesiastical lineage, he had a rather modest view of the office. After two quadrennia in the office, his modest view persisted. In 1972 he stated, "The United Methodist Church does not ordain its bishops; it consecrates them—keeping the function as an office instead of an order. . . . A Methodist bishop is simply a Methodist preacher elected to . . . administrative and spiritual responsibility by [the] church."[5] Behind his august presence was the heart of a pastor. Some in the Council of Bishops have said that he could have wielded more influence than he did, that with his well-read intellect he could have exercised his influence in more authoritative ways. He saw his role differently. He did not see himself as a catalyst. He saw himself as a mender of the breaches and a bridger of the divides.

Hunt was a mediator. By nature he did not like controversies, and he disdained polemics, particularly if he perceived them to be uninformed or biased stereotypes. He constantly sought a *via media.* When he deemed it necessary, usually for theological reasons, he would become involved in controversy. An example was his 1988 presidential address to the Council of Bishops when he strongly aligned himself with the church's position on homosexuality even though others were urging reconsideration of the position. Likewise, in 1994 in his Denman Lectures he castigated the recently emerged "Sophia" theology.

In most instances, however, he assumed the role of the irenic leader mediating between various constituencies and theological developments in the church. He was neither the catalyst nor the synthesist. He did not seek the ferment of debate, nor did he attempt to blend contrary positions into some synthetic amorphous compromise. He respected the dialectic of differences and sought mutual understanding. He sought to give an evangelical theology a fair hearing while respecting the liberal theological tradition that had characterized his formal education. He was committed to demonstrating that an essentially conservative theology did not lead to conservative or reactionary social and political conclusions. He was proud of his Wesleyan heritage, but that did not deter him from being a vocal advocate for his church's full participation in the ecumenical movement. He was utterly convinced that evangelism, social reform, and church-related higher education were neither in tension nor in competition with each other. While higher education and evangelism had their discrete distinctives and could not be absorbed into one or the other, they were necessarily interdependent. While social action and evangelism were distinct missional directions of the church, they should penetrate and inform each other as together they affirm the lordship of Christ in human life, social and personal.

Hunt placed himself at the point of possible breaches or divisions and put both mind and heart to the task of building bridges of understanding and mutual respect. Such a position of mediator between the lines can be as risky as that of a combatant in the lines. Between the lines, one can become a target from either direction. At least within the lines one can be shot at from only one direction. Between the lines, one's motives and objectives can be impugned. A mediator can be viewed as one who seeks constant neutrality. Hunt certainly was aware of the risks, and he experienced the ambiguities of being between the lines. He was nevertheless convinced that at least for some, the task of bringing the lines together, of bridging the gaps, of keeping the unity of peace within the church was a necessary ministry. Builder of bridges, mender of breaches, the mediator—in these roles Hunt made his greatest functional contribution as a bishop of the church.

"I believe," states Hunt, "the church can exist without bishops—and bureaucrats."[6] The church cannot exist, however, without people—"the people of God, saved through faith in his Son Jesus Christ, at work in the world to communicate to individuals and to society the message and meaning of his redeeming and transforming love."[7] In spite of its frailties and failures, it is the church as the people of God that God has used through the centuries to preserve and transmit the gospel. In the end, the church is the only institution on earth that exists primarily for the sake of those who are not yet in it. His baptism as an infant, his decision for Christ in late childhood, his sense of calling to the ministry in late youth, his ordination to the ministry of Word and sacrament, and his consecration as a bishop are the road signs to Hunt's varied and complex ministry. As preacher, he chooses words to bridge the gap between pulpit and pew; as educator, he revels in "the glory of the lighted mind"; as evangelist, he pushes and tugs the church into the marketplace; as mediator, he envisions a diverse church in the unity of the Spirit; and as a faithful believer, he confidently affirms:

> A charge to keep I have, a God to glorify,
>   a never-dying soul to save, and fit it for the sky
> To serve the present age, my calling to fulfill;
>   O may it all my powers engage to do my Master's will![8]

Notes

Preface

1. Katherine Hankey, "I Love to Tell the Story," *The United Methodist Hymnal* (Nashville: The United Methodist Publishing House, 1989), no. 156.
2. David J. Bosch, *Transforming Mission: Paradigm Shifts in Theology of Mission* (Maryknoll, N.Y.: Orbis Books, 1991), p. 412.
3. Donald Dayton, *Discovering an Evangelical Heritage* (New York: Harper & Row, 1976).
4. Earl G. Hunt Jr., *A Bishop Speaks His Mind: A Candid View of United Methodism* (Nashville: Abingdon Press, 1987), p. 184.

1. Beginnings

1. William B. Grove in the foreword to Earl G. Hunt Jr., *A Bishop Speaks His Mind: A Candid View of United Methodism* (Nashville: Abingdon Press, 1987), p. 10.
2. Earl G. Hunt Jr., *Recovering the Sacred* (Lake Junaluska, N.C.: Jonathan Creek Press, 1992), p. 13.
3. Interview with Earl G. Hunt Jr., Lake Junaluska, N.C., 23 June 1998.
4. See Samuel S. Hill Jr., "The Shape and Shapes of Popular Southern Piety," in *Varieties of Southern Evangelicalism*, ed. David Edwin Harrell Jr. (Macon, Ga.: Mercer University Press, 1981), pp. 87-114.
5. Hunt, "Purely Personal," in *Recovering the Sacred*, p. 18.
6. Ibid., p. 45.
7. Ibid., pp. 56-57. See also Earl G. Hunt Jr., *I Have Believed* (Nashville: The Upper Room, 1980), pp. 94-95.
8. Grace Livingston Hill, *The Seventh Hour* (Philadelphia: J. B. Lippincott, 1938).
9. Interviews with various persons in Johnson City, Tennessee, 26 June 1998.
10. Hunt, *I Have Believed*, p. 5.
11. Hunt, *A Bishop Speaks His Mind*, p. 38.
12. Boone M. Bowen, *The Candler School of Theology—Sixty Years of Service* (Atlanta, Ga.: Emory University, 1974), p. 192.

13. Interview with Hunt, 23 June 1998.

14. Hunt, "Purely Personal," p. 26.

15. Letter from Gunnar Teilmann to Hunt, 12 April 1944.

16. Letter from Hunt to Teilmann.

17. Letter from Harrison Marshall to Hunt.

2. Pastor

1. *Journal of the Holston Annual Conference,* 1944.

2. Interview with Robert F. Lundy, 23 June 1998.

3. Interview with Ben St. Clair, 23 June 1998.

4. Earl G. Hunt Jr., "Purely Personal," in *Recovering the Sacred* (Lake Junaluska, N.C.: Jonathan Creek Press, 1992), p. 20.

5. Letter from Pat Rees (Smith), 5 March 1951.

6. Hunt, "Purely Personal," p. 23.

7. Interview with Earl G. Hunt Jr., Lake Junaluska, N.C., 23 June 1998.

8. Letter to F. B. Shelton from Hunt, Emory and Henry Archives.

3. College President

1. See George J. Stevenson, *Increase in Excellence: A History of Emory and Henry College 1836–1963* (New York: Appleton-Century-Crofts, 1963).

2. Letter from Hunt to Shelton, Emory and Henry Archives.

3. Ibid.

4. Interview with George Stevenson by Robert Lundy.

5. Earl G. Hunt Jr., "Macte Virtute," in *Recovering the Sacred* (Lake Junaluska, N.C.: Jonathan Creek Press, 1992), p. 37.

6. Ibid.

7. Ibid., p. 38.

8. Ibid., p. 41.

9. Interview with Earl G. Hunt Jr., Lake Junaluska, N.C., 24 June 1998.

10. Ralph Sockman as quoted in Hunt, *Recovering the Sacred,* p. 22.

11. Emory and Henry College Archives.

12. *The Sphinx,* Emory, Virginia, 1963.

13. Quoted in Scott David Arnold, "The Integration of Emory and Henry College" (master's thesis, University of Richmond, May 1996). Arnold's research carefully draws from the college records deposited in the Emory and Henry Archives. His meticulous research has been invaluable in gaining a synoptic view of this period in the college's history.

14. Ibid.

15. Letter in Emory and Henry Archives.

16. Interview with Hunt, 23 June 1998.

17. Letter of Hunt to Edna Mae Scarborough, 1978. Over the years Hunt repeatedly paid tribute to his secretaries: Mrs. Alma Underwood and Mrs. Margaret Williams of Wesley Memorial Church, Chattanooga; Mrs. Grace Portrum of First Church, Morristown; Mrs. Wanda Teague of the Charlotte Area; Mrs. Marie Thompson of the Nashville Area; Mrs. Nina Nailing of the Florida Area; Mrs. Joretta Caldwell, Mrs. Lynda Leonard, Mrs. Freida Rhinehart, and Miss Cynthia Webb of the Foundation for Evangelism.

18. Citation filed in the Emory and Henry Archives.

4. Episcopacy

1. Episcopal Address, *The Daily Christian Advocate,* 27 April 1964, p. 15.

2. Interview with Edgar A. Eldridge by Robert Lundy, 14 July 1996.

3. William R. Cannon, *A Magnificent Obsession* (Nashville: Abingdon Press, 1999), pp. 195-96. In the same volume see Hunt's comment, p. 7.

4. Roy H. Short, *History of the Council of Bishops of The United Methodist Church* (Nashville: Abingdon Press, 1980), p. 197.

5. Earl G. Hunt Jr., *A Bishop Speaks His Mind: A Candid View of United Methodism* (Nashville: Abingdon Press, 1987), p. 151.

6. Tom H. Matheny, "Reforming Episcopal Elections," *Circuit Rider,* February 1983, pp. 15-16.

7. Earl G. Hunt Jr., *I Have Believed* (Nashville: The Upper Room, 1980), p. 163.

8. *Journal of the Western North Carolina Annual Conference,* 1976.

9. The messages from Ralph Sockman and Clovis Chappell are in the Hunt papers, United Methodist Archives, Madison, N.J.

10. Interview with John James Miller by Robert Lundy.

11. A. B. Weaver in *Old Fires on New Altars,* ed. Wilson O. Weldon (Charlotte: Institute for Homiletical Studies, Western North Carolina Annual Conference, 1972), p. 20.

12. Ibid., p. 23.

13. Ibid.

14. *Journal of the Western North Carolina Annual Conference,* 1985.

15. Quoted in Hunt, *A Bishop Speaks His Mind,* p. 60.

16. *Journal of the Western North Carolina Annual Conference,* 1968.

17. Interview with Earl G. Hunt Jr., Lake Junaluska, N.C., 24 June 1998.

18. *Charlotte Observer,* 27 July 1972.

19. *Journal of the Western North Carolina Annual Conference,* 1973.

20. Ibid.

21. Earl G. Hunt Jr., "United Methodists and Roman Catholics," in *Recovering the Sacred* (Lake Junaluska, N.C.: Jonathan Creek Press, 1992), p. 114.

22. Ibid., p. 113.

23. *Journal of the Western North Carolina Annual Conference,* 1976.

24. Letter from Julian Lindsey to James Logan, 6 August 1997.

25. Interview with Edward L. Crump Jr. by Robert Lundy, 15 July 1996.

26. *Journal of the Memphis Annual Conference*, 1979.

27. *Journal of the Tennessee Annual Conference*, 1979.

28. Hunt in his episcopal report to the Southeastern Jurisdictional Conference, found in the *Journal of the Southeastern Jurisdiction*, 1980, p. 131.

29. *The Paducah Sun*, 2 June 1980, p. 12-A.

30. *The United Methodist Reporter of the Tennessee Conference*, 23 June 1978.

31. Ibid.

32. Ibid.

33. *Journal of the Memphis Annual Conference*, 1980.

34. *Journal of the Tennessee Annual Conference*, 1980.

35. Interview with Hunt, 24 June 1998.

36. *Journal of the Florida Annual Conference*, 1981, pp. 199-201.

37. Ibid.

38. Earl G. Hunt Jr., ed., *Storms and Starlight: Bishops' Messages on the Holy Spirit* (Nashville: Tidings, 1974).

39. Ibid., pp. 12-14.

40. Ibid.

41. Interview with Bishop Joe E. Pennel Jr., 1997.

42. *St. Petersburg Times*, 20 June 1987.

43. Ibid.

44. Ibid.

45. *Journal of the Florida Annual Conference*, 1988.

5. Bridge Builder

1. James K. Mathews, *Set Apart to Serve: The Meaning and Role of Episcopacy in the Wesleyan Tradition* (Nashville: Abingdon Press, 1985), p. 176.

2. Ibid., p. 241.

3. Murray H. Leiffer, "United Methodism, 1940–60," in *The History of American Methodism*, edited by Emory S. Bucke (Nashville: Abingdon Press, 1964), 3:513-15.

4. Frederick A. Norwood, *The Story of American Methodism* (Nashville: Abingdon Press, 1974), p. 414.

5. *The Daily Christian Advocate*, 27 April 1976, Advance Edition F., "Bishop and District Superintendent Study Commission 1972–76," p. 13.

6. Quoted in Mathews, *Set Apart to Serve*, p. 241.

7. Robert Moats Miller, *Bishop G. Bromley Oxnam: Paladin of Liberal Protestantism* (Nashville: Abingdon Press, 1990).

8. Leon Smith, ed., *Homosexuality: In Search of Christian Understanding* (Nashville: Discipleship Resources, 1981).

9. *The Book of Discipline* (Nashville: The United Methodist Publishing House, 1972), p. 86.

10. Earl G. Hunt Jr., "On Being Leaders and Selecting Battle Lines," in *Recovering the Sacred* (Lake Junaluska, N.C.: Jonathan Creek Press, 1992), pp. 208-19.

11. Report to the South Carolina Annual Conference of The Methodist Church of the Committee Appointed to Study the National Council of Churches of Christ in the U.S.A., as published by the National Council of Churches.

12. Hunt wrote the article for *Interpreter,* June 1975, which was subsequently reprinted in quantity by the National Council of Churches. The quote is from "Linked in Ministry: A Bishop Examines the Work of the National Council of Churches of Christ," as published by the National Council of Churches.

13. Ibid.

14. Hunt, "Negative Response to Crises Boosts Anti-Church Forces," a statement that Hunt issued to the churches in his episcopal area.

15. Ibid.

16. Hunt, "The Day of the Lord," in *Recovering the Sacred,* pp. 130-41.

17. Ibid.

18. Ibid.

19. Ibid.

20. *The Daily Christian Advocate,* 1988, pp. 412, 614. An excellent historical account of the work of the Committee on Our Theological Task is given by Richard Heitzenrater, "In Search of Continuity and Consensus: The Road to the 1988 Doctrinal Statement," in Doctrine and Theology in The United Methodist Church, ed. Thomas A. Langford (Nashville: Kingswood Books of Abingdon Press, 1991), pp. 93-108.

21. Schubert Ogden, "Doctrinal Standards in The United Methodist Church," in Langford, *Doctrine and Theology,* pp. 39-51.

22. *Circuit Rider,* February 1987, pp. 9-15.

23. John B. Cobb Jr., "I Say, 'Keep the Quadrilateral!'" *Circuit Rider,* May 1987, pp. 4-6.

24. Kenneth C. Kinghorn, "I Say, 'The Bible Is the Decisive Source of Authority!'" *Circuit Rider,* May 1987, pp. 6-7.

25. David E. Conner, "Theological Pluralism Is Our Greatest Hope . . . ," *Circuit Rider,* May 1987, pp. 11-12.

26. Richard P. Heitzenrater, "At Full Liberty: Doctrinal Standards in Early American Methodism," *Quarterly Review* 5 (fall 1985): 6-27.

27. Thomas C. Oden, "What Are 'Established Standards of Doctrine'? A Response to Richard Heitzenrater," *Quarterly Review* 7 (spring 1987): 42-62. Oden's subsequent book was *Doctrinal Standards in the Wesleyan Tradition* (Grand Rapids, Mich.: Francis Asbury Press of Zondervan Publishing House, 1988).

28. *The Book of Discipline,* p. 75.

29. Ibid., p. 72.

30. *The Daily Christian Advocate,* 7 May 1988, p. 7.

31. Earl G. Hunt Jr., *A Bishop Speaks His Mind: A Candid View of United Methodism* (Nashville: Abingdon Press, 1987).

32. Ibid., p. 144.

33. Ibid., pp. 144-45.

34. Ibid., pp. 93-99.

35. Ibid., p. 86.

36. Ibid., p. 151.

37. John Silber in a letter to Edmund Robb, 29 August 1987.

38. William B. Grove in foreword to Hunt's *A Bishop Speaks His Mind.*

6. Preacher

1. See James D. Glasse, *Profession: Minister* (Nashville: Abingdon Press, 1968).

2. Harvey Cox, *The Secular City* (New York: Macmillan, 1965).

3. Earl G. Hunt Jr., "Purely Personal," in *Recovering the Sacred* (Lake Junaluska, N.C.: Jonathan Creek Press, 1992), p. 28.

4. Reinhold Niebuhr, *The Nature and Destiny of Man* (New York: Charles Scribner's Sons, 1949).

5. Quoted in Earl G. Hunt Jr., *A Bishop Speaks His Mind: A Candid View of United Methodism* (Nashville: Abingdon Press, 1987).

6. Ibid., pp. 107-18.

7. Ibid., p. 107.

8. Earl G. Hunt Jr., "Christ's Mighty Victory," *Good News*, October-December 1971, pp. 83-90.

9. Ibid., p. 86.

10. Ibid., p. 85.

11. Ibid.

12. Earl G. Hunt Jr., "If Morning Is to Come," *The United Methodist Reporter of the Tennessee Conference*, 23 June 1978.

13. Ibid.

14. Earl G. Hunt Jr., *I Have Believed* (Nashville: The Upper Room, 1980), p. 25.

15. Ibid.

16. Ibid., p. 155.

17. Ibid., p. 157.

18. *St. Petersburg Times*, section E, 20 June 1987.

19. Hunt, *A Bishop Speaks His Mind*, p. 112.

20. Ibid., pp. 104-5. Fosdick is quoted by Hunt from *Harper's Magazine*, July 1928.

21. Ibid., p. 113.

22. Phillips Brooks, *Lectures on Preaching* (New York: E. P. Dutton, 1877).

23. Hunt, *A Bishop Speaks His Mind*, p. 115.

24. Ibid. Source of quote not cited.

25. Ibid., pp. 117-18.

26. Ibid., p. 112.

7. Evangelist

1. Charles M. Laymon, *Thy Kingdom Come* (Nashville: The General Board of Evangelism, 1964), p. 82.

2. For the academic year 1997–1998 E. Stanley Jones Professors of Evangelism in United Methodist schools of theology were Dr. Bryan Stone (Boston), Dr. Priscilla Pope-Levison (Duke), Dr. Martin Alphonse (Garrett-Evangelical), Dr. Henry H. Knight III (Saint Paul), Dr. James C. Logan (Wesley), Dr. Roberto Escamilla (Methodist Theological School in Ohio), and the Reverend Achim Hartner (Evangelisch-Methodistische Kirche Theologisches Seminar, Reutlingen, Germany).

3. Mortimer Arias, *Announcing the Reign of God: Evangelization and the Subversive Memory of Jesus* (Philadelphia: Fortress Press, 1984).

4. Harold Rogers, *Harry Denman: A Biography* (1977; reprint, Nashville: The Upper Room, 1993).

5. Earl G. Hunt Jr. and Ezra Earl Jones, eds., *Prophetic Evangelist—The Living Legacy of Harry Denman* (Nashville: The General Board of Discipleship, 1993).

6. James C. Logan, ed., *Theology and Evangelism in the Wesleyan Heritage* (Nashville: Kingswood Books of Abingdon Press, 1994).

7. James C. Logan, ed., *Christ for the World: United Methodist Bishops Speak on Evangelism* (Nashville: Kingswood Books of Abingdon Press, 1996).

8. Earl G. Hunt Jr., "The Old Story in a New Day," in *Recovering the Sacred* (Lake Junaluska, N.C.: Jonathan Creek Press, 1992), p. 251.

9. Ibid. Hunt quotes Edwin Holt Hughes, *Evangelism and Change* (New York: The Methodist Book Concern, 1938), p. 41.

10. Earl G. Hunt Jr., *Evangelism for a New Century* (Nashville: Discipleship Resources, 1994).

11. Earl G. Hunt Jr., *I Have Believed* (Nashville: The Upper Room, 1980).

12. Ibid.

13. *The United Methodist Reporter of the Tennessee Conference,* 23 June 1978.

14. Ben Campbell Johnson, *Speaking of God: Evangelism as Initial Spiritual Guidance* (Louisville: Westminster/John Knox Press, 1991), p. 15.

15. John Westerhoff III, *Will Our Children Have Faith?* (Minneapolis: Winston Press, 1976), p. 38.

16. Earl G. Hunt Jr., *A Bishop Speaks His Mind: A Candid View of United Methodism* (Nashville: Abingdon Press, 1987), p. 106.

17. G. K. Chesterton, "The House of Christmas," as quoted by Hunt, *I Have Believed,* p. 43.

18. Earl G. Hunt Jr., "The Right Kind of Evangelism," *Circuit Rider,* February 1997, p. 8.

19. Hunt, *Evangelism for a New Century,* p. 3.

20. Leander Keck, *The Church Confident* (Nashville: Abingdon Press, 1993), p. 115.

21. Hunt, *Evangelism for a New Century,* p. 15.

22. Ibid., p. 23.

23. Ibid., pp. 62-63.

24. Hunt, "The Right Kind of Evangelism," p. 8.

25. William Abraham, *The Logic of Evangelism* (Grand Rapids, Mich.: Eerdmans, 1989), pp. 217-23.

8. Educator

1. Alexis de Tocqueville, *Democracy in America,* ed. J. P. Mayer and Max Lerner (New York: Harper & Row, 1966), p. 265.

2. Earl G. Hunt Jr., "Macte Virtute," in *Recovering the Sacred* (Lake Junaluska, N.C.: Jonathan Creek Press, 1992), p. 41.

3. Ibid., p. 38.

4. Ibid., p. 40.

5. Ibid., p. 39.

6. Ibid., p. 41.

7. Ibid.

8. Ibid.

9. Earl G. Hunt Jr., "The University's Responsibility to Church and Society," *The Emory University Quarterly,* summer 1967, p. 109.

10. Earl G. Hunt Jr., "'As If We Were God's Spies': The Critical Need for a Church-Related College," Lambuth College, Jackson, Tennessee, 2 April 1970.

11. Ibid.

12. Ibid.

13. Ibid.

14. Earl G. Hunt Jr., "In the Country of the Young," a sermon preached in Duke Chapel, 18 October 1970. Printed in the *Duke Alumni Register,* November 1970, pp. 21-26.

15. Hunt, "As If We Were God's Spies."

16. Ibid.

17. Ibid.

18. Ibid.

19. Ibid.

20. George Marsden, *The Soul of the American University: From Protestant Establishment to Established Nonbelief* (New York: Oxford University Press, 1994).

21. James Tunstead Burtchaell, *The Dying of the Light: The Disengagement of Colleges and Universities from Their Christian Churches* (Grand Rapids, Mich.: Eerdmans, 1998).

9. Believer

1. Earl G. Hunt Jr., Lake Junaluska, N.C., 8 September 1996.

2. Earl G. Hunt Jr., "Purely Personal," in *Recovering the Sacred* (Lake Junaluska, N.C.: Jonathan Creek Press, 1992), p. 20.

3. Earl G. Hunt Jr., *I Have Believed* (Nashville: The Upper Room, 1980).

4. Earl G. Hunt Jr., *A Bishop Speaks His Mind: A Candid View of United Methodism* (Nashville: Abingdon Press, 1987), p. 68.

5. Ibid.

6. Ibid., p. 110.

7. Hunt, "Christ's Mighty Victory," *Good News,* October-December 1971, p. 84.

8. Hunt, *I Have Believed.*

9. Ibid., p. 17. Hunt quotes Norman Macleod, source not cited.

10. Ibid., p. 36.

11. Ibid.

12. Ibid., p. 45.

13. Ibid., p. 46. Hunt quotes from John S. Whale, *The Right to Believe* (New York: Scribner's, 1938), p. 35.

14. Ibid., pp. 46-47.

15. Ibid., p. 49. Hunt quotes from James S. Stewart, *A Faith to Proclaim* (New York: Scribner's, 1953), p. 109.

16. Ibid., pp. 22-23.

17. Ibid., p. 56.

18. Ibid., p. 63.

19. Ibid., p. 151.

20. Ibid., pp. 160-61.

21. Ibid., p. 159.

22. Ibid., p. 164.

23. Ibid.

24. Ibid., p. 165.

25. Ibid., pp. 165-66.

26. Hunt, "In the House of the Lord Forever," in *Recovering the Sacred,* p. 224.

27. Hunt, *I Have Believed,* p. 168.

28. Hunt, Lake Junaluska, N.C., 8 September 1996.

Epilogue

1. Roy H. Short, *The Episcopal Role in United Methodism* (Nashville: Abingdon Press, 1985), p. 127.

2. William R. Cannon in the foreword to Earl G. Hunt Jr., *Recovering the Sacred* (Lake Junaluska, N.C.: Jonathan Creek Press, 1992), p. 7.

3. Francis Asbury, *The Journal and Letters of Francis Asbury,* ed. Elmer T. Clark, 2 vols. (Nashville: Abingdon Press, 1958), 2:787.

4. Cannon, foreword to *Recovering the Sacred,* p. 8.

5. Earl G. Hunt Jr., "The Episcopacy—'72 Model," message at installation for Bishop Joel D. McDavid, Lakeland, Fla., 14 September 1972.

6. Hunt, *I Have Believed.*

7. Ibid.

8. Charles Wesley, "A Charge to Keep I Have," *The United Methodist Hymnal* (Nashville: The United Methodist Publishing House, 1989), no. 413.

Index

Abraham, William, 185
Ade, George, 148
Allen, L. Scott, 70
Alleyne, C. C., 41
Allison, Fred C., 52
Alphonse, Martin, 237n
Anderson, Hugh, 147
Anselm, Saint, 151
Arias, Mortimer, 167, 171
Armbrister, Victor, 57, 61
Arnold, Scott David, 232n
Asbury, Francis, 22, 92, 114, 227
Atkins, James, 52
Atwood, Sanford, 202

Barlow, Emily Miller, 28
Barnes, James, 171
Barth, Karl, 147, 207, 211, 213, 227
Bashore, George W., 175
Beecher, Henry Ward, 145
Beecher, Lyman, 145, 157, 182
Begley, Michael J., 86
Bethune, Mary McLeod, 109, 170
Blackburn, Robert M., 111, 224
Blake, Bruce P., 175
Bolinger, Andy, 28-29
Booth, William, 127
Bosch, David, 19
Boulton, Bish. and Mrs. Edwin C., 176
Boyd, M. W., 41
Branscomb, John Warren, 99
Branson, Mark, 167
Brooks, Phillips, 145, 157
Broomfield, John Calvin, 170
Brown, Dorothy Hayes, 64

Broyles, Joseph Warren, 25-26
Brunner, Emil, 147, 211
Bryan, Monk, 174
Bryan, William Jennings, 52
Buechner, Frederick, 146
Bultmann, Rudolf, 211
Burtchaell, James T., 201
Buskirk, James, 171
Buttrick, George A., 145, 146, 210

Caldwell, Joretta, 233n
Caldwell, Kirby John, 171
Campbell, Dennis, 169, 172
Cannon, William R., 36, 47, 70, 71-72,
    117, 202, 226, 227
Carder, Kenneth L., 171, 175
Carr, Jerry B., 94
Carter, Jimmy, 118
Cartwright, Peter, 189
Castro, Emilio, 171
Cavallero, Violetta, 170
Chappell, Clovis G., 47, 74
Chesterton, G. K., 182
Clark, Roy C., 95, 224
Claypool, John, 146
Cleland, James T., 46, 147
Cobb, John B., Jr., 132
Coffin, Henry Sloane, 36
Collins, Charles, 49, 50
Conn, Harvie M., 167
Conner, David E., 133
Connolly, Phillip, 173
Corson, Fred P., 55
Cosby, Gordon, 45, 47
Cousins, Norman, 58, 60

Cowper, William, 96
Cox, Edward, 22
Cox, Harvey, 143
Craddock, Fred B., 146
Crook, James R., 174
Crump, Edward L., Jr., 93
Culberson, G. C. ("Connie"), 57
Cushman, Ralph Spaulding, 47, 170

Davis, Charles, 64
Davis, Robert A., 109
Dayton, Donald, 20
Dempsey, Jack, 39
Denman, Harry, 165, 169, 170, 172, 173, 177, 187, 227
DeVault (Hunt), Tommie Mae, 23-24, 44, 54
Dodd, M. E., 29
Dodson, Malone, 171
Dublin, Lord Mayor of, 127
Duecker, R. Sheldon, 175
Duffey, Paul A., 224
Dunlap, Dale, 136

Early, Roy E., 41
Eddy, Sherwood, 36
Edwards, Jonathan, 177
Eldridge, Edgar A., 71
Elizabeth, Queen, 171
Emerson, Ralph Waldo, 158
Emory, John, 50
English, Donald, 171
English, E. Schuyler, 29
Ensley, Francis Gerald, 79
Entler, Fred, 57
Ervin, Paul R., Jr., 176
Erwin, Richard, 83
Escamilla, Roberto, 237n
Eustler, R. Kern, 224

Fannin, Robert E., 225
Finch, Mr. and Mrs. George D., 76, 79
Finger, H. Ellis, Jr., 58, 70, 195, 202
Finney, Charles Grandison, 177, 204
Fisher, Neal F., 170
Fitzgerald, Ernest A., 84, 224
Floyd, Arva Colbert, 36
Foot, Hugh, 58

Ford, Leighton, 80
Forsyth, Peter Taylor, 145, 210
Fosdick, Harry Emerson, 145, 155-56
Fox, Eddie, 171
French, John Stewart, 46, 52
Furman, Frank, 103, 111

Galvan, Elias G., 175
Gamble, B. C., 37
Gamble, Marshall L., 27, 41
Garfield, James, 56
Gibson, Foye G., 48, 51, 53, 55
Gilgan (Hunt), Edeltraut, 44-45
Glover, T. R., 211
Golden, Charles F., 170
Golden, James Walter, 170
Goodrich, Robert E., Jr., 80
Goodson, W. Kenneth, 70
Gossip, Arthur John, 147, 210, 217
Graham, Billy, 80, 173
Gray, Mai, 130
Greer, Robert E., 42
Grenfell, Wilfred T., 87
Griffith, A. Leonard, 80
Grotius, Hugo, 151
Grove, William, 21
Gustafson, M. O. (Gus), 166

Hall, Thor, 78, 79
Hamilton, J. Wallace, 108
Hardin, Paul, III, 197
Harding, Joe A., 171, 174
Harmon, Nolan B., Jr., 34, 75
Harmon, Rebecca, 34
Harris, Harold C., 47
Harris, Marie, 47
Hartner, Achim, 237n
Havea, John, 127
Hays, Brooks, 60
Heckard, Cecil, 77
Heitzenrater, Richard, 130, 133, 134, 135, 136
Henley, James W., 99, 102
Henry, Patrick, 50
Herbert, C. C., 76
Herndon, Harold, 38
Hill, Grace Livingston, 30

Hodge, Bachman Gladstone, 65
Hooker, Richard, 129
Hopkins, Mark, 56
Hoss, Embree, 52, 115
Hough, Lynn Harold, 206
Hughes, Edwin Holt, 29, 46, 157, 177
Hughes, Hasbrouck, 168
Humphreys, Robert E., 52
Hunt, Ann, 24
Hunt, Bill, 24
Hunt, Bruce, 24
Hunt, Clara, 24
Hunt, Earl, Sr., 22-23, 44
Hunt, Earl Stephen, 44-45, 54
Hunt, Edeltraut, 44-45
Hunt, Grandfather, 24
Hunt, Homer, 24
Hunt, Mary Ann, 30-34, 44, 54, 111, 225
Hunt, Nell, 24
Hunt, Tommie Mae, 23-24, 44, 54
Hutchinson, Orion, Jr., 84

Irons, Neil L., 175
Ivey, George, 82

James, William, 97
John XXIII, 87
Johnson, Ben Campbell, 180
Jones, E. Stanley, 167, 169, 170, 227
Jones, Ezra Earl, 173

Kammerer, Charlene P., 106, 225
Keck, Leander, 183
Kelly, Frederick T., 59
Kelly, Howard Atwood, 29, 37
Kern, Paul B., 41, 43, 47
Key, William R., 174
Kierkegaard, Søren, 181
Kim, Hae-Jong, 175
Kim, Helen, 170
Kinder, Charles E., 165, 166, 167, 168, 169
Kinder, Phyllis, 169
Kinghorn, Kenneth C., 133
Kirkland, Bryant M., 79
Knight, Harold, 172
Knight, Henry H., III, 237n
Knox, J. Lloyd, 224, 225

Kramer, Russell R., 63, 71
Kulah, Arthur F., 175
Kyker, Dr. and Mrs. Charles Hartsell, 30
Kyker (Hunt), Mary Ann, 30-34, 44, 54, 111, 225

Lackey, A. Glenn, 23
Lambert, Jeremiah, 22
Lambuth, Walter Russell, 52
Lane, Mr. and Mrs. B. B., 167
Laney, James T., 111, 202-03
Langford, Thomas, 135, 136
Laubach, Frank, 60
Lawson, David J., 175
Lefever, Ernest W., 118
Leidig, Daniel G., Jr., 57, 58, 63, 64, 66, 141, 163
Leiffer, Murray H., 115
Leonard, Lynda, 233n
Lewis, Douglass, 168-69
Lewis, Edwin, 26
Lindsey, Julian A., 83-84, 90
Loder, Dwight, 127
Logan, James C., 119, 172, 237n
Lord, John Wesley, 102
Love, Edgar A., 83
Love, Eva Pollock, 111
Lowell, James Russell, 158
Luccock, Halford E., 146, 171
Lundy, Elizabeth, 40
Lundy, Robert, 37, 38, 40, 42
Luther, Martin, 204, 208

Macartney, Clarence Edward, 47
Macleod, Norman, 213
Madison, J. Clay, 83
Marcellus, Cecil H., Jr., 84
Marsden, George, 201
Marshall, Catherine, 47
Marshall, Harrison, 40
Marshall, John H., Jr., 165, 169
Marshall, Peter, 29, 210
Mason, W. C., 33, 57, 61, 63
Matheny, Tom, 73
Matheson, John Ed, 171
Mathews, James K., 175
McCallie, James Park, 29
McCleskey, J. Lawrence, 79, 225

McDavid, Joel, 99, 110
McDonell, Durward, 110
McKendree, William, 22
Miller, James Shannon, 52
Miller, John James, 75
Miller, Perry, 75-76
Miller, Samuel, 97
Minor, Ruediger R., 175
Mohney, Ralph W., 172
Moody, Dwight L., 36, 212
Moody, Paul D., 36
Moore, Arthur J., 32, 40, 104, 138
Moore, Mrs. Arthur J., 32, 40, 47
Morgan, G. Campbell, 36
Morrell, W. M., 43
Morris, William W., 95, 225
Mott, John R., 36, 47, 48, 170, 227

Nailing, Nina, 233n
Neff, William, 64
Neuhaus, Richard John, 118
Newman, Ernest W., 224, 225
Newton, Joseph Fort, 179
Niebuhr, H. Richard, 148
Niebuhr, Reinhold, 146, 148
Niles, Daniel Thambyrajah, 146, 170
Norris, Alfred L., 175
North, Frank Mason, 123
Norwood, Frederick, 116

Oden, Thomas C., 133, 134, 135
Ogden, Schubert, 129-30
Ogletree, Thomas, 131, 135
Origen, 186
Outen, George H., 171
Outler, Albert C., 129, 171, 227
Oxnam, G. Bromley, 117-18, 146, 212

Parker, Franklin Nutting, 36, 117, 147, 213
Parlin, Charles, 60
Paul, Saint, 177, 208
Pendergrass, Edward J., Jr., 70, 102
Pennel, Joseph E., Jr., 106, 225
Perry, J. W., 41
Peters, James C., 84
Pevahouse, Joe, 98-99
Phelps, William Lyon, 36

Pope-Levison, Priscilla, 237n
Porterfield, Thomas L. ("Pidney"), 57
Portrum, Grace, 233n
Profitt, Joab, 60

Raines, Richard C., 102
Ramer, Lloyd W., 94
Ramsey, Paul, 118
Read, David H. C., 210
Rees, Pat, 45-46, 47
Rhinehart, Freida, 233n
Rhodes, Stephen, 171, 176
Richardson, Emmit, 63
Richardson, G. G., 31
Rider, Ben, 103
Robb, Edmund W., Jr., 118
Robinson, John A. T., 154
Rogers, Harold, 173
Runyon, Theodore, 131

Sanders, Carl J., 70
Sanford, Terry, 196
Scarborough, Edna Mae, 65
Schleiermacher, Friedrich, 212
Schofield, Curtis, 173
Seamands, Earl Arnette, 171
Sheeley, Lynn, 47
Sheen, Fulton J., 86
Shelton, Floyd B., 48
Sherer, Ann B., 175
Sherman, Frank W., 108, 111
Sherman, Mrs. Frank W., 108
Sherrod, Charles C., 63, 71
Shirakawa, Tatsumasa (Ted), 37
Shirkey, Albert P., 47
Short, Roy H., 48, 56, 72, 99, 116, 226
Silber, John, 139
Sloan, Harold Paul, 29
Small, R. Leonard, 80
Smart, W. Aiken, 36, 117
Smith, O'Dell, 46
Smith, Wilbur, 102
Sockman, Ralph W., 47, 59, 60, 74, 125, 146
Spain, Robert H., 99, 224, 225
Speer, Robert E., 29, 36
St. Clair, Ben, 42, 43, 174, 202
Stanley, Samuel A., Jr., 38

Stebbins, George C., 36

Stevenson, George, 55

Stewart, James S., 79, 146, 147, 161, 210, 215

Stockton, Thomas B., 224

Stokes, Mack B., 36, 47, 202, 203

Stone, Bryan, 237n

Straughn, James Henry, 115

Stuart, "Jeb", 52

Taylor, Joseph E., 174

Teague, Wanda, 233n

Teilmann, Gunnar, 37, 38, 39, 40

Teilmann, Wava, 40

Terhune, Albert Payson, 152

Thielicke, Helmut, 147, 211

Thompson, Marie, 233n

Tillich, Paul, 154, 211

Tittle, Ernest Fremont, 146

Tocqueville, Alexis de, 190

Trimble, Henry Burton, 36, 37

Troeltsch, Ernst, 185

Trotter, F. Thomas, 204

Trueblood, Elton, 60

Tullis, Edward L., 14

Tunney, Gene, 39

Turkington, Charles G., 174

Tuttle, Robert G., Sr., 75

Tuttle, Robert G., Jr., 170

Underwood, Alma, 233n

Vanzant, Roland, 110

Waites, James, 111, 169, 203

Walker, Alan, 171

Wall, James, 119

Weatherhead, Leslie, 214

Weaver, Charles C., 56

Webb, Cynthia, 233n

Weldon, Wilson, 77, 78

Wesley, Charles, 186, 190

Wesley, John, 86, 105, 107-8, 127, 129, 160, 172, 177, 186, 189, 204, 205, 208, 227

Westerhoff, John, 180

Whale, John S., 215

White, Charles D., 76

White, Woodie W., 175

Wilder, James, 42

Wilke, Richard B., 175

Williams, Margaret, 233n

Yeakel, Joseph H., 175

Young, H. Claude, Jr., 84